Careful attention to the text and perceptive pastoral application, all laced with disarming humor, is a rare combination in a commentator. But Dale Ralph Davis regularly employs such a combination to wonderful effect. Down to earth, this commentary provides solid devotional content for the Christian. Packed full of help on how the Old Testament is good for us as Christians, it provides an excellent example of how to handle Ezra-Nehemiah for the preacher. Its striking simplicity is undoubtedly accomplished through an intimacy with the text and breadth of research (hinted at in the footnotes). This commentary is a gift to Christ's church – vintage Dale Ralph Davis.

S. D. Ellison
Director of Training, Irish Baptist College, Belfast, Northern Ireland;
author, *Raised According to the Scriptures: Easter in the Old Testament*

In characteristic fashion, Davis provides a studied and clear commentary filled with pastoral insight and even a humorous anecdote here and there. I strongly commend this volume for anyone who desires to understand Ezra–Nehemiah and hear a word of hope in the midst of hardship.

William M. Wood
Associate Professor of Old Testament,
Reformed Theological Seminary, Atlanta, Georgia

T0356821

FOCUS • ON • THE • BIBLE

EZRA & NEHEMIAH

THE QUEST FOR RESTORATION

DALE RALPH DAVIS

CHRISTIAN
FOCUS

Scripture translations, unless indicated otherwise, are the author's.

Scripture quotations marked (AV) are taken from *The Authorised (King James) Version (AV)*, Crown copyright.

Scripture quotations marked (ESV) are taken from *The Holy Bible, English Standard Version*. Copyright © 2001 by Crossway Bibles, a division of Good News Publishers. Used by permission. All rights reserved.

Scripture quotations marked (NASB) are taken from the *New American Standard Bible*®. Copyright © 1960, 1962, 1963, 1968, 1971, 1972, 1973, 1975, 1977, 1995 by The Lockman Foundation. Used by Permission. (www.Lockman.org)

Scripture quotations marked (NIV) are taken from *The Holy Bible, New International Version*®. NIV®. Copyright©1973, 1978, 1984 by International Bible Society. Used by permission of Zondervan. All rights reserved.

Scripture quotations marked (NJPS) are taken from the Tanakh: A New Translation of the Holy Scriptures according to the Traditional Hebrew Text (1985).

Scripture quotations marked (RSV) are taken from the *Revised Standard Version* of the Bible. Copyright © 1952 [2nd edition, 1971] by the Division of Christian Education of the National Council of the Churches of Christ in the United States of America. Used by permission. All rights reserved.

Dale Ralph Davis is a renowned Bible teacher who lives in rural Tennessee. He has been a pastor in various churches and was Professor of Old Testament at Reformed Theological Seminary, Jackson, Mississippi.

Copyright © 2025 Dale Ralph Davis

Paperback ISBN 978-1-5271-1224-7

E-book ISBN 978-1-5271-1289-6

10 9 8 7 6 5 4 3 2 1

Printed in 2025
by
Christian Focus Publications Ltd.,
Geanies House, Fearn, Ross-shire,
IV20 1TW, Scotland, U.K.

www.christianfocus.com

Cover design by MOOSE77

Printed and bound by
Bell & Bain, Glasgow

Contents

Abbreviations

AB	The Anchor Bible
ABD	Anchor Bible Dictionary
ASV	American Standard Version (1901)
AV/KJV	Authorized/King James Version
BST	The Bible Speaks Today
CC	Concordia Commentary
EBC	The Expositor's Bible Commentary
ESV	English Standard Version
GW	God's Word (World, 1995)
HCSB	Holman Christian Standard Bible
ISBE	International Standard Bible Encyclopedia
LXX	The Septuagint
NAC	New American Commentary
NASB	New American Standard Bible
NCBC	New Century Bible Commentary
NICOT	New International Commentary on the Old Testament
NIDOTTE	New International Dictionary of Old Testament Theology & Exegesis
NJB	New Jerusalem Bible
NJPS	Tanakh: A New Translation of the Holy Scriptures according to the Traditional Hebrew Text (1985)
NRSV	New Revised Standard Version
NT	New Testament
OT	Old Testament
REB	Revised English Bible
REC	Reformed Expository Commentary
RSV	Revised Standard Version
TOTC	Tyndale Old Testament Commentary
WBC	Word Biblical Commentary
ZECOT	Zondervan Exegetical Commentary on the Old Testament
ZPEB	Zondervan Pictorial Encyclopedia of the Bible

Preface

When friends asked about my writing of late, I told them the world was waiting for another commentary on Ezra and Nehemiah. Naturally that's nonsense. Not even the church is waiting for that. Ezra and Nehemiah rate pretty low on the scale of the church's biblical interest. One can understand why. Think of the historical setting – these were hardly the giddy days of the kingdom of God. Then think of the prime characters. Ezra is a rather 'flat' character, who hardly fires the imagination. Admittedly, Nehemiah stirs the juices of some. He is far more colorful than Ezra (Ezra pulled out his own hair, Nehemiah pulled out other people's hair!). So, the church likes to co-opt Nehemiah for a bit to use for its principles-of-leadership gigs. Then too, there may be too much realism about the 'people of God' in these books. The upshot is this is not the most well-traveled chunk of holy writ.

So what about this commentary? Well, I have tried to do adequate 'dirty work' in the text but to cast it in an expository form to give the illusion of order, without being allergic to illustration or a bit of application. Perhaps a word on illustrations. I think they are helpful for grasping a principle contained in the text. Most of mine come out of my 'down-time' reading, which tends to gravitate to history and sports. Some readers may find that irritating, or, as some might say, off-putting. If so, the solution is simple: don't buy the book. I won't be hurt, and the publishers will still be solvent. Translations of the biblical text are my own unless specified otherwise.

I send forth this study as a last tribute to the memory of my father, James Daryl Davis. He was captive to the Scriptures.

He thought the King had spoken – and so no pains should be spared over his Word. For the psychologically curious, we did not have a close emotional relationship, but over the years I increasingly realize what a massive impact – often more like a stream flowing underground – my father's attitude and sweat over the Word of God has had on me. I must not be remiss in giving thanks to the Giver.

DALE RALPH DAVIS
After Easter 2024

Sketchy Preliminaries

Welcome to Persia! It is post-539 B.C., a time in biblical history known as the post-exilic period. Remember that the last contingent of the people of Judah was carted off to Babylon in 587 B.C. But on 29 October 539, Cyrus came into the city of Babylon in peace, and Persia was the head-knocker of the world.

One could do worse than to live in a Persia-dominated world. Persia was very eager to show her subject peoples that 'the government is *for* you.' Well, that may be a bit of exaggeration. We shouldn't think that Cyrus, for example, was as warm and cordial as a used car salesman. He well knew how to use fear, terror, and intimidation.[1] And yet the Persians were ecumenical in their religious policy. They encouraged subject peoples to worship their own gods/goddesses, and, generally, they did not deport and relocate captive populations. As captors went, Persians were somewhat temperate. According to Hoerth, under the Persians Palestine was, along with Phoenicia, Syria, and Cyprus, now grouped into a Persian district called 'The Land Beyond the River' [the Euphrates], with Damascus as its capital. Palestine itself was sectioned into provinces: Galilee, Samaria, Judah, and Idumea.[2]

So much for Persian policy. Now meet her leading politicians. You'll encounter most of these kings in Ezra and Nehemiah, so it will be useful to have a checklist of them for handy reference:

---

1. See Susan Wise Bauer, *The History of the Ancient World* (New York: W. W. Norton, 2007), 461-62. For a very readable overview of the Persian empire and history, see Bauer, 455-68, 500-46; for more detail, cf. Edwin M. Yamauchi, *Persia and the Bible* (Grand Rapids: Baker, 1990), 65-278.

2. Alfred J. Hoerth, *Archaeology and the Old Testament* (Grand Rapids: Baker, 1998), 389.

Cyrus II	559–530
Cambyses II	529–522
Darius I	522–486
Xerxes I (Ahasuerus)	485–465
Artaxerxes I	464–424

Finally, let me provide an overview of these books. There seems to be good reason to suppose Ezra and Nehemiah were originally considered one book,[3] though there are some who want to treat them as distinct documents.[4] Here I am treating them as a unified document.

The text contains what seems to be pretty dry stuff – lists, reports, letters, archives, and yet it is cast into a narrative framework that falls into four defined sections: (1) Ezra 1–6, from Cyrus' decree to the rebuilding of the temple; (2) Ezra 7–10, the coming of Ezra and reforms under his direction; (3) Nehemiah 1–6, the coming of Nehemiah and rebuilding of the city walls; and (4) Nehemiah 7–13, the re-structuring of the community's life. Time-wise Ezra–Nehemiah takes up a little over a hundred years, from Cyrus' decree (c. 539 B.C.) to Nehemiah's second tenure in Jerusalem (c. 433 B.C.). There is one dominant focus in each block of material. In the following outline the sub-points will suggest the flow of thought within each section. I suppose a rubric, like 'Tenacious hope in tough times,' would catch the tone of the whole. Hence …

I. The New Temple, Ezra 1–6

1. A future and a hope, ch. 1
2. The founders of the renewed Israel, ch. 2
3. A new beginning … and a new song, ch. 3
4. Do not wonder, brothers, that the world hates you, ch. 4
5. The King's decree and the kings' decrees, chs. 5–6

---

3. B. S. Childs, *Introduction to the Old Testament as Scripture* (Philadelphia: Fortress, 1979), 626.

4. See Andrew E. Steinmann, *Ezra and Nehemiah*, CC (St. Louis: Concordia, 2010), 12-21.

II. The New Rule, Ezra 7–10

1. Enjoying the hand of God, chs. 7–8
2. Escaping the wrath of God, chs. 9–10

III. The New City, Nehemiah 1–6

1. The good hand of my God, chs. 1–2
2. The careful record of my workers, ch. 3
3. The great opposition to my work, chs. 4–6

IV. The New Society, Nehemiah 7–13

1. The work of reformation, chs. 7–10
2. The work of consolidation, 11:1–13:3
3. Always reforming?, 13:4-31[5]

Now, on to the text.

---

5. Much of this section has been regurgitated from my book *The Word Became Fresh* (Ross-shire: Christian Focus, 2006), 87-88. For a helpful orientation to Ezra–Nehemiah as a whole, especially its theology, see George Van Pelt Campbell, 'Structure, Themes, and Theology in Ezra–Nehemiah,' *Bibliotheca Sacra* 174 (Oct-Dec 2017): 394-411.

EZRA

1

History Mover

(Ezra 1)

Unsuccessful athletic teams don't generate much enthusiasm. Not all readers will care a lick about American professional baseball, but … time was when the St. Louis Browns and the Washington Senators were extant – and they were almost perpetually losers. Their very names were synonymous with failure. In my childhood I lived within sixty miles of Pittsburgh, Pennsylvania, but the Pittsburgh Pirates seemed married to seventh place (next to last) in the league standings. Losers don't stir attention. And Israel was a loser. The big powers were Babylon, then Persia – and who cares about a postage-stamp size fief in the political backwater of the Near East? Or the people who used to live there? Only a covenant God does. Because he has made promises to these losers, and so he will move history on their behalf. That's the undertow in Ezra 1 – *God moves history to give his people a future and a hope.*

We may be in the Book of Ezra but in Ezra 1–6 we are still in pre-Ezra time, and the book opens about 538 B.C. or so with a decree of Cyrus, King of Persia, and we find ourselves face to face with **the political providence of God** (vv. 1-4, and perhaps vv. 5-6 as well).

But there's something before the 'political': 'And in the first year of Cyrus, king of Persia, to fulfill the word of Yahweh from the mouth of Jeremiah, Yahweh stirred up the spirit of Cyrus, king of Persia, so that he made proclamation throughout all his kingdom and also put it in writing' (v. 1).[1] Notice the major concern: to fulfill Yahweh's Word through Jeremiah. The text is referring to Jeremiah 29:10-11:

> For thus says the LORD: When seventy years are completed for Babylon, I will visit you, and I will fulfill to you my promise and bring you back to this place. For I know the plans I have for you, says the LORD, plans for welfare and not for evil, to give you a future and a hope (RSV).

And to the likes of Jeremiah 25:11-12:

> This whole land shall become a ruin and a waste, and these nations shall serve the king of Babylon seventy years. Then after seventy years are completed, I will punish the king of Babylon and that nation, the land of the Chaldeans, for their iniquity, says the LORD, making the land an everlasting waste (RSV).

Jeremiah had had to pound into the heads of the people of Judah that the exile to Babylon would be no passing affair. There were scuzzball prophets, appealing to the people's desires, who predicted that Judah's exile would be quite brief, that the exiles would soon return, and that 'normalcy' would reign in Judah again (cf. Jer. 28). No, not on your life, Jeremiah countered. It will last seventy years, *then* Yahweh will bring you back. And the first verse of Ezra says, 'Well now, Jeremiah was right, wasn't he?' Indeed, that's why Yahweh 'stirred up' Cyrus – in order to fulfill the previous word he had spoken. So the providence here is an 'assisting' providence – it is in the service of the word. Providence sees that promises come true.

But the 'providence' was blatantly political, and one doesn't just see that in the report of verse 1 ('Yahweh stirred up the spirit of Cyrus, king of Persia, so that …') – the idea permeates the proclamation itself:

> Here's what Cyrus king of Persia says: 'Yahweh, God of heaven, has given to me all the kingdoms of the earth and **he** has charged me to build for him a house in Jerusalem, which is in Judah.

---

1. Cyrus reigned over Persia before this; the 'first year' here refers to his conquest of Babylon.

Whoever (is) among you from all his people, may his God be with him and let him go up to Jerusalem, which is in Judah, and let him build the house of Yahweh God of Israel – he is the God who is in Jerusalem. And every survivor from all the places where he sojourns, let the men of his place support him with silver and gold and goods and livestock, along with a free-will offering for the house of God, which is in Jerusalem' (vv. 2-4).

But someone will object, 'Surely you don't think Cyrus actually thought this way about Yahweh?' Probably not. 'Surely this is a bit of Persian propaganda?' Probably so. But no need to get one's bowels in an uproar. Think of what likely took place. Cyrus directs someone in his Office for Jewish Affairs to draft the requisite document. He tells him what he wants to express, tells him to write it up, and he'll sign off on it. What a delightful assignment!

So our Jewish bureaucrat has Cyrus saying that 'Yahweh, God of heaven, has given to me all the kingdoms of the earth.' Cyrus doesn't blink to allow such 'theology,' but our Jewish ghost-writer has just had him confess Yahweh's universal sway and sovereignty. Moreover, Yahweh is 'God of heaven' (v. 2) and yet 'the God who is in Jerusalem' (v. 3b). He is both 'up there' and 'down here,'[2] both omni-competent yet locatable, both high above yet terribly near. It's ironic and rather amusing: Cyrus intends to express a political policy, and his Jewish editor helps him confess orthodox truth. In any case, it all took place because 'Yahweh stirred up the spirit of Cyrus' to allow any of Israel's exiles to return to Jerusalem with community support. It was more than Persian policy – it was Yahweh's providence, a 'political' providence. Yahweh is not afraid to get his hands mixed up in politics.[3]

---

2. Robert Fyall, *The Message of Ezra and Haggai*, BST (Downers Grove, IL: Inter-Varsity, 2010), 34.

3. The climactic verse of one of Isaiah's prophecies, namely Isaiah 44:28, predicts of Cyrus what Ezra 1:1-4 says he did. Many critics hold that that prediction did not come from Isaiah but from a much later hand, because, whether they confess it or not, they don't believe there can be genuine supernatural predictive prophecy, especially 160 years ahead of time. See John Oswalt's discussion (*The Book of Isaiah: Chapters 40–66*, NICOT [Grand Rapids: Eerdmans, 1998], 192-97) on how only the assumption of genuine predictive prophecy fits the *theological argument* of Isaiah 40–48. Josephus (*Antiquities*, xi.i.1-2) claims Cyrus had read Isaiah's predictions and so sought to act in accord with them. But Josephus can

While on this theme of providence, note that verses 5-6 point to an *overflowing* providence as well. More was needed than 'stirring up' the spirit of Cyrus (v.1) – God also had to stir up the exiles and their leadership to be willing to return to Jerusalem. He did that and also encouraged them in the venture by the generous support provided by those around them, perhaps even from their pagan neighbors (v. 6). It was a sort of re-enactment of how the Egyptians enriched Israel when they left Egypt (Exod. 12:35-36). And likely the people desperately needed to be 'stirred up.' By this time (538 B.C. or so), two generations of Israel had grown up knowing no home but Babylon and having had no memory or experience of Judah and Jerusalem.[4] What could move them to face a hazardous journey, an unfamiliar destination, and quite possibly a tenuous, from-scratch existence – in Judah? But these were people 'whose spirit God had stirred up.' He was not merely dealing with Cyrus but goading his own people to restore their heritage.

Now let's come back to this main idea of 'political' providence. In all the maze of the world's turmoil and devastation and confusion, does the living God really move and motivate and direct leaders and nations? Sometimes even men of the world seem to think so. In 1943, William MacKenzie King, the Canadian prime minister, told Winston Churchill that no one else could have saved the British empire in 1940 as Churchill had. Churchill replied that he had had exceptional training in having been through a previous war and having much experience in government. To this King replied, 'Yes, it almost confirmed the old Presbyterian idea of pre-destination or pre-ordination; of his having been the man selected for this task.' Conservative politician Lord Hailsham put it even more directly: 'The one case in which I think I can see the finger of God in contemporary history is Churchill's arrival at the premiership at that precise moment in 1940.'[5] The Bible doesn't need human support, but it is

---

be flaky, and one must keep a healthy dose of skepticism within reach when weighing his claims.

4. E.g., Fyall, 37.

5. Andrew Roberts, *Churchill: Walking with Destiny* (New York: Viking, 2018), 2.

interesting that sometimes even men of this age recognize God's 'political' providence.

Clearly, in our text the welcome change for Israel is not primarily due to Cyrus' policy but to Yahweh's providence, to the God who 'stirs up' Cyrus. All this is not really so surprising for the Most High who rules the kingdom of men and gives it to whom he will (Dan. 4:17, 25, 32). Here is a rump people – and a God who runs history for their benefit. 'So we are always of good courage' (2 Cor. 5:6).

Secondly, notice how central **the chosen city of God** is in this chapter. Cyrus' decree said that Yahweh had charged him 'to rebuild him a house in Jerusalem' (v. 2, NASB). Here would be something 'foreign' to the exiles, for they 'had never seen or experienced the temple and its worship.'[6] But Jerusalem is mentioned seven times in this chapter (vv. 2, 3 [2 t.], 4, 5, 7, 11), usually in connection with the house/temple to be built there.

Before the Babylonians had decimated Jerusalem in 587 B.C., the prophet Jeremiah had been trying to hammer into King Zedekiah's skull that the Babylonians were indeed going to devastate Jerusalem (Jer. 37:8; 38:3, 18, 23; 39:8). Now it looks like it may receive new attention. But even in the scheme of biblical prophecy Jerusalem always seems to have a fresh future. In the eighth century (700s B.C.) Micah had prophesied that

> Zion will be turned into a ploughed field,
> Jerusalem a heap of ruins,
> and the temple mount an overgrown height (3:12).

But then, in the very next section, Micah says that 'at the end of the days' (4:1) 'many nations' will come to Yahweh's mountain and house to be instructed, 'for torah [law, instruction] will go forth from Zion and the word of Yahweh from Jerusalem' (4:2). A heap of ruins at one time but down the road in the future the source of Yahweh's Word to converted nations. Indeed, the prophet Zechariah (prophesying in this Persian restoration period but in the pre-Ezra generation) relates Yahweh's assurance that he will 'again choose Jerusalem' (Zech. 1:17)

---

6. Derek W. H. Thomas, *Ezra & Nehemiah*, REC (Phillipsburg, NJ: P & R, 2016), 9.

and that he 'has chosen Jerusalem' (3:2). The import is that even a bit of Jerusalem's future has begun in this rather minor restoration under the Persian regime.

The whole tone of this 'Jerusalem' emphasis suggests the dogged tenacity of Yahweh, who simply refuses to trash and nuke the people he has originally laid hold of. It may mystify us, but we've seen the like in other venues. Time was when our oldest son was in toddler time and prized a stuffed rabbit he called 'Cardy.' Time took a toll on Cardy. He/it was light brown but his original 'fur' was pretty much gone over a good bit of his body. One could see the crisscross of the base fabric everywhere. But, as is often the case with kids, there could be no thought of consigning Cardy to the disposal he clearly merited, and there could be real distress if this ravaged rabbit happened to be misplaced and temporarily unfindable. One just didn't surrender Cardy. But it's a similar tenacity, it seems, that Yahweh has. He simply refuses to let go of Jerusalem, insists on 'again choosing Jerusalem,' and the repeated mention of it/her in Ezra 1 points to this unfazed fidelity of Yahweh toward her. And this kind of God is one in whom we can always rest.

There is a third emphasis in our chapter, what I would call **the solemn humor of God** (vv. 7-11). The text seems anything but 'humorous,' however, because it is primarily an inventory. So we must begin with that.

What then is here? An accounting of the articles from Yahweh's temple that Nebuchadnezzar had pilfered and placed in the sacred precincts of Babylon. Nebuchadnezzar had done this in 605 B.C. (see Dan. 1:1-2; cf. 2 Chron. 36:7) as well as in 587 B.C. (2 Kings 25:13-15; Jer. 52:17-19). Victors might cart off images of the deities of a conquered people, but there were no images of Yahweh, so the 'sacred stuff' from his temple had to suffice. But now Cyrus, with his more benevolent policy, was restoring these temple vessels, and so Mithredath, his treasurer, itemizes them to Sheshbazzar, Judah's leader.

We do meet up with some obscurities in the listing in verses 9-11. In verse 9 there are 29 of something – duplicates, knives, censers – whatever. And then in verse 10 there are 410 silver bowls 'seconds' – whatever that means. Then the total given in verse 11 (5,400) is far above the sum of the individual entries. Who knows why? One possibility is that the list is selective and not exhaustive, while the total is comprehensive.

This inventory also points to what is fulfilled. The shadow of Jeremiah from verse 1 still hangs over this chapter, though the text here does not directly mention him. In Jeremiah 27:16-22 the prophet was denouncing the optimistic prophets who predicted that in the very near future the temple vessels Nebuchadnezzar had carted off to Babylon would be returned. Instead, Jeremiah insisted that even more temple goods would be carried off to Babylon:

> To Babylon they will be carried and there they will be until the day I pay attention to them, says Yahweh; then I shall bring them up and bring them back to this place (v. 22).

This prophecy 'covered' both the vessels taken in 605 B.C. (Dan. 1:1-2) and those pilfered in 587 B.C. Such was the word through that badgered, beaten, belittled prophet Jeremiah. And now as Mithredath counts out the temple vessels one by one (v. 8), we are seeing the accurate fulfillment of Jeremiah's prediction.

But where is the 'humor' here? Well, it is certainly 'solemn' and low-key, but let me try to explain.

Let's go back to 605 B.C., when Nebuchadnezzar, king of Babylon, took off the first wave of exiles into captivity. These included Daniel and his friends. Daniel 1:1-2 says that on that occasion 'the Lord gave' not only King Jehoiakim into Nebuchadnezzar's power but also 'some of the vessels of the house of God,' and Nebuchadnezzar spirited them off to Babylon and placed them 'in the house of his god [or, gods]'. He stashed them 'in the treasure house of his god.' Now there is no doubt how ancient media moguls would view this. The meaning was clear: the defeated god's 'stuff' was in the victorious god's precincts. Marduk had bested Yahweh. The latter, it would be held, was unable to protect his people, his city, and his relics. That was the media 'take.'

There was more shame than this, however. Years later, just before Babylon fell, Belshazzar held a great feast; he and his nobles were boozing themselves under the table (Dan. 5:1). Then he ordered that the vessels from the temple in Jerusalem

– the ones Nebuchadnezzar had captured – should be brought
so that the nobles and ladies might drink from them. So
they 'drank wine, and praised the gods of gold and silver,
bronze, iron, wood, and stone' (Dan. 5:4, RSV). Desecration
in excelsis! But now these flagons that Belshazzar and his
wives and whores had sloshed around and slobbered over
were being returned to their rightful people and place.

But this had happened before, where the humor was much
more obvious. The story is in 1 Samuel 4–6. Israel had taken
the ark of the covenant into battle with the Philistines – they
were sure that if they had Yahweh's furniture, they would
have Yahweh's help (1 Sam. 4:3). But it didn't work that way.
Alas, the Philistines won anyway *and* captured the ark. They
put the ark before the image of Dagon in the Ashdod shrine.
Once more the news outlets all said the same thing: the ark
of the 'defeated' Yahweh was in the presence of the victorious
god, Dagon. Next morning, however, Dagon's image was
sprawled on its face in front of Yahweh's ark (5:3). The 'victor'
was doing obeisance to the 'loser'! The biblical writer must
have had a smirk on his face as he penned verse 3b: 'So they
took Dagon and put him back in his place.' Next morning,
worse scenario – Dagon lies splattered before the ark and
his head and his hands have been broken off. Repeated
performances tend to be fatal! Dagon is getting the godness
knocked out of him. The symbolism is clear: Yahweh is the
real victor, Dagon merely the victim, which becomes crystal
clear when a plague follows the ark wherever they take it
in Philistia (5:6-12). Clearly, Dagon was unable to protect
his people from Yahweh's ravages. The upshot was that the
Philistines sent the ark back to Israel. Well, not exactly. They
had it ready to go but decided on a little test. They hooked
up to their cart two never-yoked cows who'd recently had
calves, and took their calves away from them and shut them
up. They said that if the cows and cart went up the road to
Israel, it would be a sure sign that Yahweh had brought the
plague on them. Such cows would normally return to their
calves but these went up to Israel, bellowing as they went,
in protest over leaving their calves. It was as if an unseen
hand was forcing them to go up to Israel. There is both biting
humor and clear revelation in that story. Part of the revelation

is: Yahweh, unlike Dagon, does not need his people to prop him up; he brought back his ark *all by himself.*

Back to Daniel 1 and Ezra 1. In this case, Yahweh did not act quite so 'independently.' This time he 'stirred up' Cyrus to restore the pilfered vessels (Ezra 1:1, 7). When we hear Mithredath say, 'Okay ... gold dishes ... twenty-eight, twenty-nine, thirty,' don't you sense that the Lord's 'shame' of Daniel 1:2 is in the process of being reversed? It's *solemn* humor, but it's humor nonetheless. He's the God who deals in reverses, who restores honor where once there was shame.

Of course, this 'reversal' pattern operates not only in God's case but in the lives of his people as well. Think of the stigma that stuck to William Farel and John Calvin when they were banished from Geneva after Easter 1538. In the following months life in Geneva became more chaotic and undisciplined. Then a change in political leadership took place. Calvin, who had been flourishing in Strasbourg, eventually received the 'bad news' that Geneva was begging him to come back. To Calvin, Geneva was a 'place of torture' and yet in September 1541 he returned, and in his preaching took up the very next biblical passage he would have preached in 1538 – if he had not been run out of town. Calvin was not thrilled to be back in Geneva. But it was one of the Lord's reverses, turning shame into honor. The Lord frequently does this for his people. And it really is rather humorous.

2

What You Can Discover in the Church Roll
(Ezra 2)

I attended a college in the middle of the state of Kansas. The wind always blew there; if from the south, weather would generally be fair; if from the north, cold or blustery. I recall one day, with a south wind, it was 78 degrees (Fahrenheit). The very next day, with wind from the north, it was 13. That's similar to the jolt a reader receives when going from Ezra 1 to Ezra 2. In Ezra 1, we're in a reasonably interesting narrative, when, upon passing into Ezra 2, we are, rather abruptly, hit with a tedious list that goes on and on. Why does the Bible do that to us? As you read verses 12-15 – 'the sons of Azgad, 1,222; the sons of Adonikam, 666; the sons of Bigvai, 2,056; the sons of Adin, 454' – do you find they stir your devotional juices, give you a warm glow inside? What are we to make of this?[1]

A bit of advice: don't gripe. The reason: the Bible is being kind to you. In what way? Well, did you notice that Ezra 2 does not give you the names of returnees but only of *groups* of them, almost always referring to 'the sons of so-and-so'? So think how *condensed* this list is! What if every one of the family of Parosh (v. 3) was listed and you had to read through 2,172 names, until you got to the sons of Shephatiah (v. 4) only to run into 372 more? We wouldn't care to get hit with 30 to

---

1. Nehemiah 7 is a parallel passage but differs in some details from Ezra 2. We can put off discussion of such matters until we come to Nehemiah 7.

40,000 names. So the writer spares us that. He categorizes folks under the names of their ancestors (vv. 3-20) or locale (vv. 21-35), for example. So, in Ezra 2 we do not have a massive mess but a controlled condensation. Gratitude is in order.

Still, we must ask what we are to make of this rather pedantic (to us) list. Let's take verses 1-35 first, which point us to **the stubborn continuity of the purposes of God.** And note the introductory comment in verse 1: 'And these are the sons of the province coming up from the captivity of the exile, whom Nebuchadnezzar king of Babylon had exiled to Babylon – and they returned to Jerusalem and Judah, each one to his city.'

But why did these 'come up' from captivity, why did they return to Jerusalem? This was a sizable but not a humongous contingent of people. Most of the exiled Jews stayed in exile, where they enjoyed a 'relatively hospitable way of life in Babylon' and didn't have to face 'the grim prospects of beginning life again in a land of dust and ashes.'[2] So why would these returnees return? Why would they even think of going back to Judah? After all, they were for the most part two generations removed from the disaster that befell Judah in 587 B.C. Most of them had never laid eyes on Judah or Jerusalem. The permission of Cyrus (1:1-4) might have encouraged them. Yahweh's promises of 'a future and a hope' may have moved some (Jer. 29:10-14). Or, perhaps, as 1:5 puts it, it was simply that God had 'stirred [them] up.' In any case, we owe a tribute to these people for what they were willing to venture.[3]

---

2. Eugene H. Merrill, *Kingdom of Priests* (Grand Rapids: Baker, 1987), 473.

3. In more recent years Jews have responded enthusiastically when offered the opportunity to return to the land. Edwin Yamauchi includes a fascinating comment in his exposition: 'Modern experiences in repatriating Jews to Israel have consistently shown enthusiastic responses in large numbers when such opportunities were presented. The first of these efforts was "Operation Magic Carpet," which in 1950 airlifted fifty thousand Yemenite Jews to Israel. At one time, Baghdad was one-fifth Jewish. "Operation Ezra and Nehemiah" in 1951 and 1952 transported one hundred thirty thousand Iraqi Jews to Israel, which severely depleted the number of Jews in the country. There are fewer than twenty Jews living in Baghdad and fewer than one hundred in Iraq. Operation Moses airlifted fourteen thousand Falashas, the Black Jews of Ethiopia, to Israel in 1985. A second airlift, called "Operation Solomon," brought fourteen thousand more Falashas to Israel. Operation Exodus in 1989 brought more than seven hundred thousand Jews out of the Soviet Union

Babylon (cf. v. 1) no longer dominates the Near East, and Zion is about to be renewed, and here is the tally, both in terms of *people* (vv. 3-20) and *place* (vv. 21-35). Returnees are listed either in their connection with a specific ancestor or their residence in a particular town in the land. These 'people' and 'place' elements, however, point us back to the 'Abraham Plan,' in Genesis 12 and following. Yahweh had announced a four-pronged promise to Abram/Abraham in Genesis 12, which can be summarized this way:

People [seed]
    'I will make you into a great nation' (v. 2)
    'To your seed …' (v. 7)

Protection / Presence
    'I will bless your blessers and the one despising you
    I will curse' (v. 3a)

Program
    'In you all the families of the ground will be
    blessed' (v. 3b)

Place
    'To the land that I will show you' (v. 1)
    'To your seed I will give this land' (v. 7)[4]

The 'people' and 'place' elements of this promise are both underscored in this tally in Ezra 2. What seems a rather dull list nevertheless points to the ongoing validity of the Abraham Plan in both its 'people' and 'place' components. You may think that after all that has occurred – the destruction of Jerusalem, the various waves of exile, the passage of years – you may think that the 'plan' has been shelved indefinitely and allowed to run down the historical drain. But no, the stubborn God of the Bible won't let it happen. So here are the *people*, sons of Parosh – and Elam and Adin and Hashum and more – and others who settle at certain addresses in the *land*.

---

to Israel' ('Ezra and Nehemiah,' EBC, 13 vols. [Grand Rapids: Zondervan, 2010], 4:400; hereafter cited as Yamauchi, EBC, vol. and page number).

4. See my book *The Word Became Fresh* (Ross-shire: Christian Focus, 2006), 32-43, for more discussion.

Yahweh's promises have a certain inevitability about them even in dark times.

That is a note that Frances Cleveland once struck. She was the young, beautiful, and popular wife of President Grover Cleveland, who had lost his bid for re-election and so, in March 1889 the Clevelands were having to leave the White House. As one of the staff escorted Frances to her departing carriage, Mrs Cleveland exhorted him to take excellent care of all the White House furnishings. She said she wanted everything ship-shape for the time 'when we come back again.' The caretaker was surprised at such talk and asked 'jus' when does you-all expec' to come back?' She smiled. 'We are coming back just four years from today.' And they did.[5] Cleveland was elected again after a four-year hiatus. She spoke as if it was, well, inevitable. And that is the hallmark of Yahweh's promises, even centuries-old ones. That's why when Jesus says, 'I will build my church' (Matt. 16:18), we never lose heart.

Secondly, this list implies something about **the reigning priority of the people of God** (vv. 36-58, 68-69).

Notice, for example, verses 36-39, where four clans of priests appear with their respective tallies. The total of the four of almost 4,300 constitutes approximately 10 per cent of the total returnees, according to verse 64. One in ten of the returnees was a priest. Why so many priests? Doesn't this suggest the apparent interest of the priests in re-establishing and serving in the temple worship? Wouldn't they come because they longed to serve at the altar in a restored temple – something they could never do in exile?[6] Is it really a stretch to assume that they longed to restore the public worship of God so they could serve where they were meant to serve?

Then, too, we can't help but note the faithful presence of those we might dub 'lesser servants' (vv. 40-58). The Levites,

---

5. Paul F. Boller, Jr., *Presidential Wives* (New York: Oxford, 1988), 174.

6. Think of Ezekiel, who was among the 'second wave' of exiles taken to Babylon in 597 B.C. If the '30th year' of Ezekiel 1:1 refers to the prophet's own age, what a disappointment he faced. The 30th year was likely the age when a priest could begin to serve (cf. Num. 4:30), yet he is marooned in Babylon, never to serve in the Jerusalem temple, much as perhaps he may have anticipated doing so.

for instance. Probably all those in verses 40-42 were Levites, but Kidner is probably right that those in verse 40 directly assisted the priests (seventy-four of them; cf. Num. 3:5-10).[7] That's one Levite to every fifty-eight priests. Those are precious few Levites to do the chores and guard duty and assist in tasks connected with temple worship. That 'lesser' role may have provided little incentive for Levites to return. But seventy-four did.

Then we come to the tally of the temple servants (*nethinim*) in verses 43-54. These were appointed long since by David to assist the Levites (see 8:20), probably with various temple-related chores. They were, status-wise, a rung below the Levites. And the 'sons of Solomon's servants' are added to these temple servants. Their role may have been the same but perhaps they had been appointed by Solomon as supplementary to the temple servants. In any case, both groups are tallied together – 392 of them (v. 58).

Finally, note the generous contribution of the congregation reported in verses 68-69. Note how the text says they arrived 'at the house of Yahweh' – even though it hadn't yet been rebuilt; and their gifts were for 'the house of God' in order to restore it. The whole focus was on restored worship. If the gold darics were the Persian daric, 61,000 darics would equate to 1,133 pounds of gold, and 5,000 minas of silver to 6,300 pounds.[8] The number of slaves in verse 65 in light of the total returnees in verse 64 indicates there was about one slave for every six freemen – which implies some of the returnees must have had a degree of wealth.[9] And they lavished it on the temple project. We must also remember that some who did not return nevertheless made substantial contributions (see 1:4, 6).

What to make of all this? What does it tell us? Simply that whether we think of the priests who were eager to serve in a restored temple, or the presence of functionaries of lesser status, or of the overflowing generosity of gifts 'for the house of God,' it all shows that the 'reigning priority' of these people

---

7. Derek Kidner, *Ezra and Nehemiah*, TOTC (Leicester: Inter-Varsity, 1979), 39-40.

8. See Yamauchi, EBC, 4:401-2. Nehemiah 7 has a different break-down of gifts.

9. Kidner, 44.

was focused on the worship of Yahweh. It's as if nothing matters more than worship.

Should one want to get picky, one might ask if there's not a subtle correction here for the church in our day. Sometimes there's such a clutter in worship itself. A worship leader or minister, wanting to project affability, opens the assembly with 'Good morning!' There is a dilatory response. He clears his throat and says, 'Let's try that again!' This time there's a more robust reaction. But if we're there to worship, do we need to mess with inane greeting lines? Or at some point in the service, often near the beginning, people are told to 'take time' and greet those around them. It may lead to five minutes of semi-chaos, depending on the church. Yes, we want folks to feel welcomed. But there is usually time before worship when any member with a concern to welcome visitors can speak to them, and there is usually plenty of time either before or after worship to visit, greet, or inquire of fellow church members. Why must we dilute the worship of God with a bunch of glad-handing? Why are we really there? And sometimes one wonders if worship is what draws folks to a church, or if they're attracted because it brandishes a hyper-kinetic youth program for one's kids. We often seem to have anemic interest in being in the sanctuary, beholding Yahweh's power and glory (cf. Ps. 63).

Finally, our 'church roll' highlights **the commendable response among the assembly of God** (vv. 59-63). This section is a kind of footnote to the record of those who returned. From five locations, apparently in Babylonia (v. 59a), were three groups (v. 60) who 'were unable to prove their ancestry or descent – whether they were from Israel' (v. 59b, Steinmann). Moreover, there were three groups of priests (v. 61) who could not authenticate their descent and so had to be excluded from serving as priests for the present (vv. 62-63).

That is the situation. But what can be missed here is that even though these folks (whether lay or priestly) had this connectional doubt hovering over them, *they still came.* They have this wobbly status but they still come. They may not have the official imprimatur of 'Israel' stamped on them, they may not be permitted to serve as priests, but that did not keep them from coming to Jerusalem. If others who 'converted' to Israel's faith could be welcomed (see 6:21), surely these who claimed Israelite descent but without sufficient proof could join the worshiping people. Nothing keeps them from acting as Israelites. The priest claimants may not be permitted priestly jobs, but they can yet be a part of the worshiping community.

Here is something instructive for us. Sometimes one bumps into folks who are willing to serve Christ's church if they have a 'ministry' in worship or music or teaching or administration, but if not, they easily fade or lose interest or peel off from the worship and teaching of the church – or remain malcontent therein. If they do not have some status as being 'recognized,' they have little interest in being a mere worshiper in Jerusalem.

Iain Murray tells of a very moving visit he had with Martyn Lloyd-Jones in the latter's very last days. Lloyd-Jones said to Murray, 'People say to me it must be very trying for you not to be able to preach – No! Not at all! I was not living upon preaching.'[10] What matters far more than any particular 'service' I may render is whether 'my soul has longed for – yes, fainted for – the courts of Yahweh' (Ps. 84:2). How grateful we should be for these unauthenticated 'Israelites' who came back to Jerusalem *anyway*.

---

10. Iain H. Murray, *The Life of D. Martyn Lloyd-Jones 1899–1981* (Edinburgh: Banner of Truth, 2013), 451.

3

Gray Days in the Kingdom of God
(Ezra 3)

Esme Duncan, originally from Aberdeen, tells of her bouts with loneliness and depression. Thankfully she had a discerning GP who suggested she might have 'Seasonal Affective Disorder,' SAD for short, a disorder that affects some folks as winter approaches and days shorten, a sort of November-to-February regimen that abets unhappiness and depression.[1] In this passage the sky is gray and everything seems so bleak. Now I am not saying that the returned exiles had a corporate case of SAD. But things must have appeared rather dreary to them. Here is a Jewish remnant returned from Babylon in 538 B.C. or so, but they come back to a devastated city with no temple and likely to a neglected countryside. They were apparently somewhat hopeful, but this was hard; they were encouraged enough to come back but starting from scratch was no picnic; they were met with hostility (v. 3); they were hardly thriving on the fumes of optimism. So we can say that Ezra 3 gives us a view of gray days in the kingdom of God. What do we meet with in such 'gray days'?

First of all – and in line with one emphasis in Ezra 2, we see **the primacy of worship** (vv. 1-6). Verse 2 highlights this point:

---

1. See Irene Howat, *Finding God in the Darkness* (Ross-shire: Christian Focus, 1998), 143. This little book is worth its weight in gold for giving us a realistic view of the Christian life.

Then Jeshua son of Jozadak and his brothers, the priests, rose up, along with Zerubbabel son of Shealtiel and his brothers, and they built the altar of the God of Israel to offer up burnt-offerings on it, in line with what is written in the torah of Moses, the man of God.

The focus is on the altar not on the temple (cf. v. 6) at this point. They begin here. But let's momentarily switch our attention a bit from the worship to the worshipers. How do they appear?

They are *fearful:* 'And they set the altar upon its base, for fear was upon them because of the peoples of the lands, and they offered upon it burnt-offerings to Yahweh, burnt-offerings morning and evening' (v. 3). Their worship was apparently stimulated because of the hostility and intimidation of the peoples around them.[2] These surrounding peoples did not want the exiles here. We've met this altar-in-hostility pattern before, both with Abram (Gen. 12:6-7) and Joshua (Josh. 8:30-35). 'Each of these prior altar-building events occurred in the context of real or potential enemies.'[3] That is usually the case. Worship occurs as a 'nevertheless' in the face of the world's pressure. It's a matter of believers staring the world in the face and saying, 'We have an altar' (Heb. 13:10) and 'we will worship in spite of you.' In Ezra 3 it seems the fear of the peoples drove Israel to worship. Nothing wrong with that. Where better to be driven than to one's Defender?

They are also *faithful* worshipers. Note the stress in verses 2 and 4: 'They built the altar ... to offer up burnt-offerings on it, *in line with what is written* in the torah of Moses,' and they celebrated the Feast of Booths *'in line with what is written.'* Their worship closely adhered to what the Bible required. This was no easy affair. Celebrating the Feast of Booths (v. 4) would require, according to Numbers 29:12-38, seventy-one bulls, fifteen rams, one hundred and five male lambs, and eight

---

2. Instead of 'because of,' some translate 'although' (a 'concessive' use of the particle *ki*); see Andrew E. Steinmann, *Ezra and Nehemiah,* CC (St. Louis: Concordia, 2010), 207. If it's causal, the fear stimulated their altar-building; if it's concessive, the fear is the context in which they built it.

3. W. Brian Aucher, 'Ezra,' in *ESV Expository Commentary*, 12 vols. (Wheaton, IL: Crossway, 2020), 4:48.

male goats![4] Worship 'by the book' could be demanding and expensive. So they kept the Feast of Booths (or, Tabernacles) because it was the seventh month (see v. 1; see Lev. 23:33-34). But they also established the normal regimen of sacrifices and offerings (vv. 5-6) – all this with the altar, before laying even the foundation of the temple (v. 6b).

These first two marks of the worshipers are instructive: fearful and faithful. They tell us that we can be fearful and faithful at the same time.

Now these worshipers are also *fragile*. I am implying this from their celebration of the Feast of Booths (v. 4). This festival was meant to remind Israel of their experience going through the 'vast and fearful' wilderness (Deut. 1:19) in post-Egypt time. During the week of this festival Israel was to live in lean-tos and huts, which conjured up vividly their precarious days in the wilderness (Lev. 23:39-43), bringing to mind how fragile life was. It was almost as if God was saying, 'That is often the situation of my people; don't ever forget that your life hangs by a mere thread.' So the Feast of Booths, or Wilderness-Reminder Week, was Yahweh's built-in annual reminder that Israel's (and our) lives can often be bleak, uncertain, and apparently insecure, and that he is our only manna (Exod. 16) and water supplier (Exod. 17). Strange, isn't it, how God often makes us combine worship with fear and uncertainty?

What then are verses 1-6 saying to us? Here the remnant in Judah is saying that *worship matters more than anything else.* And yet a bit more than that. For verses 2-3a tell us that they made a beginning – they did that when conditions were not ideal, when not everything in their corporate lives was 'all together.' But they did what they could at the time. They could build the altar. They could start there. They could worship. Sometimes the Lord works that way. He does not provide us with a full-orbed, worked-out program. Sometimes he only gives us a 'Begin here' sign.

I recall a seminary student who was grossly behind on his assignments – not only for my class but for a number of his other classes. Papers were due, and he hadn't worked on them

---

4. cf. Robert Fyall, *The Message of Ezra and Haggai*, BST (Downers Grove, IL: Inter-Varsity, 2010), 59.

or written them. He was one of my 'advisees.' One day during
this morass he came in and told me he had worked out a scheme
and overall schedule that he could follow and thereby complete
all his past-due work. I despaired. Instead of wasting time
sketching out his omni-plan, why didn't he simply go home
(or to the library) and begin writing his systematic theology
paper? Why couldn't he *start* somewhere? That at least is what
Israel did here in Ezra 3. There was no temple yet. The temple's
foundation was not even laid. But they built the altar. They did
what they could. They could worship.

Again, and happily, in the 'gray days' we meet with
the wonder of restoration (vv. 7-11). It may not look much
like restoration, but if we wade through the text I think
we will see it.

In this section we are beyond the altar and are looking at
the laying of the temple's foundation (v. 10). There are three
segments here: preparation (v. 7), organization (vv. 8-9), and
celebration (vv. 10-11). They had to have materials, and Cyrus'
benevolence was a gift horse:

> They paid the hewers and craftsmen with money, and the
> Sidonians and Tyrians with food, drink, and oil to bring
> cedarwood from Lebanon by sea to Joppa, in accord with the
> authorization granted them by King Cyrus of Persia (v. 7, NJPS).

Then management and oversight were essential: they appointed
the Levites to supervise both work and workmen (vv. 8-9).[5]

The foundation is laid, the celebration begins: priests with
trumpets, Levites with cymbals, and all with praise (vv. 10-11).
Note, however, the *lyrics* of the praise.

We've heard these lyrics before in the Old Testament: 'for
he is good; for his steadfast love lasts forever to Israel' (v. 11).
But I especially want to direct attention to the occurrence
of these words in Jeremiah 33:11. In Jeremiah 33 Yahweh
was going to show the prophet 'great and hidden things'
(v. 3) and most of those hidden things had to do with the

---

5. The text of verse 9 may be damaged; it is very difficult. But my main
contention is unaffected. Generally and earlier, the Levites' term of service began
at age twenty-five (Num. 8:23-26), but during David's time and after this was
reduced to twenty (1 Chron. 23:24, 27, and here in Ezra 3:8).

restoration he was going to bring in the future to the rack and ruin of Jerusalem. The passage even looks forward to messianic times (vv. 15-16), but some of it could certainly occur before such times. That likely includes Jeremiah 33:11. There Yahweh promises that life will come back to 'normal' in the devastated cities of Judah – folks will celebrate at weddings again and come with praise to Yahweh's house. What sort of praise? Well, they will give thanks to Yahweh, 'for Yahweh is good, for his steadfast love lasts forever.' Are the worshipers in Ezra 3 deliberately picking up the lyrics of Jeremiah 33:11? It's the same refrain. If they *are* tying into Jeremiah 33, then they are implying that the 'impossible' promised in that passage is beginning to happen, for they themselves have taken up the 'restoration refrain.' Jeremiah 33:6-13 seemed too good to be true, but the song the remnant picks up here suggests that restoration has begun.

How likely is something like this to happen? How likely is it that a people could be carted off to a foreign land and then that a cohesive portion of that people get to return to their own land fifty or more years later? Against all human likelihood God's people see God's goodness again. He is a God who restores – and not only from massive disasters like Babylonian captivity. How many of his worn-down people can testify of his restoring work in their devastating personal circumstances, that with Yahweh 'weeping may come stay in the evening, but at morning a shout of joy' (Ps. 30:5). He's the God who 'will restore to you the years that the locust hath eaten' (Joel 2:25, AV).

Finally, we see **the shadow of disappointment** (vv. 12-13) falling upon the page. Here is quite a mixed response! From verse 12b it looks like the memory of the first temple clouded the day. Some of the older folks could still recall the magnificence of Solomon's temple (1 Kings 5–7), and they could tell from the foundation of this projected temple that it would have none of the 'pizazz' of Solomon's. So their very audible mourning blended with the ecstatic joy of others to produce a weird cacophony of confusion.

The text seems to carry no rebuke for their weeping but perhaps it implies a danger may lurk in it. It's all right to register disappointment – but take care how you handle it.

In 1953 my father purchased a new car, a 1953 Chevrolet. (Obviously, I was very, very young at the time!) Functioning in his typical, characteristic mode, he selected the most basic, stripped-down, economical model. He bought the '150' model (the mid-level style was called the '210,' the most lush model was the 'Bel Air'). The 150 model had black rubber instead of chrome trim on the back fender. It was a two-door coupe – a four-door cost more. There was no radio – one didn't *need* a radio in a car. It had only regular, small hubcaps – no 'wheel covers.' And, of course, it had a 'straight stick,' no 'Power Glide' or automatic transmission. It was just dependable transportation.

Like the 'temple weepers,' it's easy for the church to be dismissive of the '150 model.' Our TV and media-driven mentality can easily think that if it's not loud or glitzy or brassy or dynamic it's of little moment. Worship that is low-key and ordinary, and plain and simple, tends to disappoint us. The amplifiers must be turned up; we need video clips to supplement the preached Word. Or take another twist. In some circles there may be much stress on Revival (not 'revival meetings' but God-sent revival), harking back to repeated revivals in history.[6] But we may so focus on 'Revival' that we forget it is possible to be faithful even if God doesn't send it. We can still engage in family worship, sincere public worship, loving intercessory prayer, and consistent Christian living in school or workplace or home. Don't despise 'the day of small things' (Zech. 4:10). We really can live in and through the gray days in the kingdom of God – the gray days can yet be faithful days.

---

6. And there have been many. Take a look at Tom Lennie's *Land of Many Revivals* (Ross-shire: Christian Focus, 2015).

4

A Whole Gob of Trouble
(Ezra 4)

The message of Ezra 4 can be summed up in a one-liner: 'Do not be surprised, brothers, if the world hates you' (1 John 3:13). We are still with the returnees from exile after 538 B.C. or so, as they proceed to work on the rebuilding of the temple.[1] Ezra 4 depicts how the world hates the Lord's people; we'll put our main heads in the second person.

First, verses 1-3 show that **the world subversively hates you**. It is a subtle 'hatred' – it approaches with a smile (v. 2):

> Then they drew near to Zerubbabel and to the heads of the fathers' [houses] and said to them, 'Let us build with you, for like you we seek your God, and we have been sacrificing to him from the days of Esar-haddon king of Assyria who brought us up here.

We have, they claim, a long history of sharing the same faith as you. But our writer knows better: he calls them 'the adversaries of Judah and Benjamin' (v. 1). He sees through their ecumenical appeal.

Indeed their very words make us wary. They allude to having been brought – apparently to the area of Samaria to the north – by Esar-haddon who reigned from 681–669 B.C. But we know of other such Assyrian deportations, for example,

---

1. The text switches from Hebrew to Aramaic at 4:8, so that 4:8–6:18 are in Aramaic; and 7:12-26 is also in Aramaic.

those under Sargon II in *c.* 720 B.C. when he brought in other peoples to settle in the area of Samaria (see 2 Kings 17:24-41). These folks practiced religious amalgamation. The writer of Kings sarcastically says, 'They feared Yahweh and they went on serving their own gods' (2 Kings 17:33). There's no reason to believe that these people had evolved into orthodox Yahweh worshipers by the time of Ezra 4. They were well-established syncretists.[2]

Zerubbabel and co. gave this offer the stiff-arm: 'You have nothing in common with us in building the house of our God, but we alone will build to Yahweh, God of Israel, as King Cyrus king of Persia commanded us' (v. 3). They base their refusal in part on a strict interpretation of Cyrus' authorization. Cyrus had directed *them*, the returned exiles, to rebuild the temple; his decree had not included others. At the same time, one senses that the exiles had theological reasons for rejecting this proposal.

In our mushy and convoluted times, the Jews' refusal here might well be called hard, harsh, and hateful. It might, in some quarters, even be dubbed a 'hate crime.' Why be so narrow and nasty toward a desire to cooperate? But sometimes God's people cannot pander or negotiate. The point here is that the Jews seemed to smell the danger. They see that separation is urgent. There are times when narrowness and intolerance is the way to spell faithfulness, when conviction must trump compromise.

Ronald Wallace tells a fascinating story in his *Readings in 1 Kings.* There was, he says, a man living in a bungalow in India when one of the great rivers was in flood. The flood was so pervasive that he found himself in his bungalow garden on a small 'island' with wide surrounding fields of water. And there in the water, swimming towards him, he saw a large and beautiful tiger. As it reached the man's island refuge it seemed relieved and rather fawning, and he was tempted to welcome it. But wisdom won out, and he took his gun and shot it dead. Sometimes the reaction must be radical – and the Jews recognized that this subversive appeal was only the wrapping of paganized syncretism. And they said no.

---

2. For further background, see Yamauchi, EBC, 4:408-9.

The church pays dire consequences when such 'subversive' hatred is not recognized and rejected. Iain Murray has written of the tragedy of the Free Church of Scotland in the latter half of the nineteenth century. Some Free Church scholars accepted the claims and dictates of German 'higher criticism' of the Bible and so surrendered belief in the historical reliability of the Bible (among other matters). Some were more devious (like A. B. Davidson) and others more open (like George Adam Smith and Marcus Dods) about accepting an error-ridden Bible. The mantra was that one could still hold gospel faith even with a fallible Bible and that, after all, one's faith is in a person and not in a book. It could all be made to look so plausible. But Marcus Dods let slip the real truth in a private letter, when he wrote:

> The church won't know themselves fifty years hence. It is to be hoped some little rag of faith may be left when all's done.[3]

Sometimes the opposition is fair-sounding and therefore subversive and therefore lethal.

Secondly, our chapter claims that **the world blatantly hates you** (vv. 4-5). In verses 1-3 the enemies approach under a guise of cordiality, but, when rebuffed, they let loose their whole arsenal:

> So the people of the land kept discouraging the people of Judah and kept frightening them about building and kept hiring counselors against them to frustrate their plans all the days of Cyrus king of Persia and on into the reign of Darius king of Persia (vv. 4-5).

In one sense this can be puzzling. Verse 4 begins with 'So ...' or 'Then ....' You can see the sequence. The people of Judah make a faithful response in verse 3 and it leads to nothing but trouble. Like Joseph in Genesis 39 – he is faithful in resisting Mrs Potiphar's invitation to bed and ends up getting thrown into the slammer.

But the primary stress here is on the withering nature of this hostility campaign. There are three Hebrew participles

---

3. Iain H. Murray, *A Scottish Christian Heritage* (Edinburgh: Banner of Truth, 2006), 386.

in these verses indicating continuous, ongoing activity: 'kept discouraging ... kept frightening ... kept hiring ...' This opposition was unrelenting; it went on non-stop. 'Discouraging' is, literally, 'making the hands drop'; the 'frightening' was likely some kind of physical threat, perhaps of armed force – some kind of intimidation. Then they kept hiring anti-Zionist lobbyists to work the halls of government back in Persia. The kingdom of Persia had a network of informers, so such paid propagandists fit right in. Suspicion, suggestion, innuendo, lies – the usual stuff in the echelons of government, to stifle, if possible, the Jews' temple project.

Here, however, the opposition is not subtle as in verses 1-3, but blatant: sheer, undisguised hostility. It is still that way. Just from a page or two of a recent prayer guide, I read of Islamic jihadists in Mozambique who boast that they had 'captured five Christians and slaughtered them, praise be to God.' Then in the Democratic Republic of Congo, Muslim extremists kill fifteen people in attacks on three villages; a pastor and his two sons are gunned down by Islamists in Plateau State, Nigeria. Open, undeterred hatred.

God's people have every right to be sad and sorrowful over this, but we also must manage a certain *shocklessness* over it as well. Jesus has told us, 'You will be hated by all on account of my name' (Mark 13:13). So, no place for surprise.

Finally, our writer wants to stress that **the world unceasingly hates you** (vv. 6-23, 24). And before wading through this section, let's be a bit pedantic and provide a list of Persian kings and their dates to have as a checklist as we move through this discussion:

Cyrus II	559–530
Cambyses II	529–522
Darius I	522–486
Xerxes I	485–465 (= Ahasuerus)
Artaxerxes I	464–424

I mainly want to discuss material in verses 6-23 and its function, but before doing that, let's touch on some scattered details.

There seem to be three accusations sent off in verses 6ff. In verse 6 itself the enemies sent an 'accusation' against the Jews to Xerxes. No details are given. We do know that after the death of Darius in 486, Egypt rebelled, and Xerxes had to march west to quell the revolt.[4] *If* the accusation in verse 6 alleged that Judah might be in revolt at this time, one can imagine why the Persians might be concerned, when already having an Egyptian revolt on their hands. Too much trouble in the west.

I take the Artaxerxes of verse 7 to be Artaxerxes I (464–424); the letter mentioned here must have been an accusation but was not spelled out. However, the third communique is laid out fully (vv. 11-16).[5] Rehum and co. express their concern (Jews rebuilding city, v. 12), worry over the fall-out from this (vv. 13, 16), affirm their own loyalty (v. 14), and make their request (v. 15; please check out the character of this city in the records). Typical political smooth-talk with its flattery, fawning, innuendo, and apparent concern for Persian interests.

Persian administration seemed efficient. Letters could travel between Samaria and Persia in about a week.[6] The search results supported the accusations. Perhaps they discovered the revolt of Hezekiah against Assyria (2 Kings 18:7) and/or Zedekiah's rebellion against Babylon (Jer. 52:3ff.). In any case, Jerusalem's urban renewal was to be nipped in the bud (vv. 17-22).

Now we come back to *the function of verses 6-23.* These verses seem to interrupt the flow of events. Verses 1-5 report opposition in the time of Cyrus and into the reign of Darius; then in verses 6-23 we read an ongoing description of opposition to Judah *down through the years,* and yet in *verse 24* we are wrenched *back* to the early reign of Darius. If we read in *chronological* order, we would read verses 1-5, then verse 24, then verses 6-23. What has happened? Well, it's as though the writer, who is relating the earlier days after the return from exile, begins telling us about the opposition Judah faced right from the first and then decides that he will simply go on (as if he's 'on a roll') and pile up all the opposition Judah

---

4. Yamauchi, EBC, 4:411.

5. In 4:9 Steinmann insists that all the 'rest of their associates' are ethnic terms: Dinaites, Apharsatheites, Tarpelites, Persians, Erechites, Babylonians, Susanites, Dahavites, Elamites; see his *Ezra and Nehemiah*, CC (St. Louis: Concordia, 2010), 236, 238-39.

6. Mervin Breneman, *Ezra, Nehemiah, Esther,* NAC (Broadman & Holman, 1993), 104.

had had through the years – so he simply keeps noting this accusation, that opposition, down through Artaxerxes' reign. But, at verse 24, it's as if he says, 'Now we need to go back to the time period that my record here in Ezra 4 is really concerned about; let's get back to 520 B.C., early in Darius' reign, when the work on the temple had ground to a halt because Judah seemed under so much duress.'

This non-sequential order, however, is not deceptive, for the writer gives clear indicators (giving us the names of the respective kings) so that we can keep the chronology straight. Moreover, the *specific objects of construction* also help us detect the different situations. Note especially verses 12-13, where the people of Judah draw fire for rebuilding the *city* and its *walls*, not the temple as in verses 1-5 and 24.[7] *Anyway*, at verse 24 we are back at the *temple* and back in the early reign of Darius (*c.* 520 B.C.). You must remember that verses 6-23 constitute a sort of big bracket piece, breaking up the chronology of chapter 4. The writer does this for *topical* reasons. He wants to overwhelm you with a sense of the *unceasing opposition* Judah has faced through all these years, as if he says, 'You might just as well see the whole sorry glob of it.' Opposition is relentless.

I can't help but think of James and Marti Hefley's book, *By Their Blood*, with its subtitle, 'Christian Martyrs of the Twentieth Century.'[8] Obviously, the scale and scope are far broader than Ezra 4. But the impression is similar. After reading over 600 pages of the hatred and hostility of earth's regimes for the servants of Christ, one sadly and obviously concludes that this animosity never ceases. But what use is that to us? It provides a dose of realism. It may sober up an all-too-eager disciple who has never realized that the life of foxes and birds may hold luxuries that one following the Son of Man never sees (Luke 9:58). Jesus thought we needed to know this stuff. He tells us, 'I have said all these things [about how the world hates you, ch. 15] to you to keep you from falling away' (John 16:1, ESV). Forewarned is forearmed.

---

7. The opposition in verses 8-23 under Artaxerxes was effective in bringing the city project to a stop. It may have been that because of their lack of security the people of Judah wanted also to rebuild the city and walls but were doing it without explicit and official authorization – and so their enemies reported and exposed them.

8. Second edition, published by Baker, 1996.

5

Getting Off Dead Center
(Ezra 5–6)

If you have a helping of peach cobbler in front of you, you naturally think how nice (and proper) it would be to have two scoops of vanilla ice cream on top of it. You can eat either by itself but, if one has the cobbler, one tends to long for the ice cream as well. I treated chapter 4 by itself – I felt I had to do that because of the amount of material. But, strictly speaking, like our erstwhile desserts, chapters 4–6 more properly belong together. There's a kind of idiom that occurs near the start of chapter 4 (4:4) and at the end of chapter 6 (6:22); in the former it is 'making the hands of the people of Judah drop,' and in the latter 'to strengthen their hands.' You won't, of course, find it like that in more recent English versions, for they translate it according to sense ('discouraged,' 'encouraged,' or the like). But if one goes back to the AV/KJV or the ASV of 1901, it's there in all its beautiful literality. It may have been placed deliberately near the beginning and at the close of chapters 4–6 in order to contrast, in bookend or 'envelope' style, the state of the people as they tried to rebuild the temple. However, we now have enough in chapters 5–6 to occupy us.

The movement of our passage develops over three main 'chunks.' We could sketch it this way:

- Prophecy and providence, 5:1-5
- Report and response, 5:6–6:12
  Request for documentation, 5:6-17

Discovery of Cyrus' decree, 6:1-5
Re-decree, 6:6-12

- Restoration and rejoicing, 6:13-22

Throughout the passage one meets repeated vocabulary: 'house of God,' naturally, something like sixteen times (5:2, 8, 13, 15, 16, 17; 6:3, 5 [2 t.], 7 [2 t.], 8, 12, 16, 17, 22) and 'decree' (Aram. *te'em*) about ten times (5:3, 9, 13, 17; 6:3, 8, 11, 12, 14 [2 t.]).

Remember the immediate historical background to our chapters (4:1-5, 24). Somewhere about 536 B.C., work on the temple ground to a halt through opposition and intimidation. That went on until the second year of Darius' reign (4:24), 520 B.C. Then the people of Judah got off 'dead center.' How do we explain the turn-around?

The first answer is that **prophecy moves us** (5:1-2; with the 'us' I'm assuming current believers can identify with the returned exiles). In the second year of Darius (4:24), during the temple-rebuilding shutdown, the prophets Haggai and Zechariah 'prophesied to the Jews who were in Judah and Jerusalem' (v. 1), which stirred Zerubbabel and Jeshua and others to action to 'rebuild the house of God which is in Jerusalem' (v. 2).

We need to flesh out this 'prophesying.' For one thing, at the first it was a *severe* word. Now, it's true that Zechariah, for example, had prophesied encouragement, citing Yahweh's words: 'I shall return to Jerusalem with compassions; my house will be built in it … and a measuring line will be stretched over Jerusalem' (Zech. 1:16). But Haggai, especially, raked the people over the coals, afflicting the comfortable. It had been something like sixteen years of lethargy over the temple project with all sorts of excuses for why the time was not right to rebuild it. So Haggai asks them if it's time for them to live in their panelled and furnished houses while Yahweh's temple lies in ruins (Hag. 1:4). He exposes their screwed-up, crypto-idolatrous priorities and tells them to 'go up to the hills, and bring timber, and build the house' (Hag. 1:8).

Sometimes that negative word, that 'critical' word must come first. Helmut Thielicke once told of how he would take his students for a weekend to one of Germany's special spots, a little village in Baden. The attraction was Urban, the village priest. Thielicke billed him as a combination of primitive Christian and comedian. With his deep bass voice one imagined he was hearing one of the ancient prophets. Seems that once, Urban decided to take two evenings to speak on 'Law and Gospel.' The first evening consisted of a judgmental sermon so ferocious and intimidating that many did not show the next evening when he spoke in much 'softer and milder terms' on the gospel. But during the previous judgment sermon, Urban had repeated as a sort of refrain: 'Even the savior first has to bash your heads in!'[1] We would prefer something a bit more restrained and refined, but you get the picture. Sometimes the Lord must expose our folly before he can encourage us in faithfulness. And in 520 B.C. he especially used Haggai to deliver a needed 'devastating' word.

This prophetic word, however, was also an *energizing* word: it moved Zerubbabel, Jeshua and the others so that they 'rose up and began to rebuild the house of God' (v. 2). As if the prophetic word carried them to obedience. We tend to forget this. It is easy to think that God's Word is a mere word, a bare word. But that is not so. Paul said he was so thankful that when the Thessalonian believers received the gospel, they 'received it not as the word of men but as it really is, the word of God, *which is also at work in you who believe*' (1 Thess. 2:13). It is not a dead word but a lively word, one that percolates and energizes in those who receive it. There is the Word, but there is also a secret power at work with it. They both go together. In principle it's something like what Faith Cook tells of John Stuart, a young merchant in west Scotland, in Ayr, about 1600 and after. He offered hospitality to John Welsh, the new minister, and would often join him, along with another friend, in times of prayer. John Stuart suffered all his life from a serious speech impediment, so severe that sometimes others could scarcely understand him. But we're told that 'whenever Stuart prayed in public, he seemed to be given relief from his handicap and attained a remarkable clarity of speech.'[2]

---

1. Helmut Thielicke, *Notes from a Wayfarer* (New York: Paragon House, 1995), 103.

2. Faith Cook, *Samuel Rutherford and His Friends* (Edinburgh: Banner of Truth, 1992), 53-54.

Strange and fascinating, isn't it? Prayer – and fluency. The two went together. And so with the Word – there is the Word *and* its being at work in believers, an energizing word, a word that stirs, rouses, and motivates, as here in verses 1-2.

Secondly, the temple project succeeded because – as the returnees would likely say, **providence surrounds us** (5:3–6:15). And one could describe this, first of all, as a *negative* providence (5:3-5). I shall explain that shortly.

It looked like there might be more trouble when Tattenai and Shethar-bozenai *et al.* came investigating, asking about who gave the Jews authorization for this building project.[3] But the tone of this inquiry does not seem hostile, like those of chapter 4. Their questioning is more objective and not threatening. They do report to King Darius but not in a vicious vein. They tell (1) of their discovery of the temple project and of questioning the Jews involved in it (5:6-10); (2) of the Jews' response with historical background and appeal to a decree of Cyrus (5:11-16); and (3) with a request that a search be made in the government archives to find the Cyrus decree (5:17).[4]

---

3. Tattenai appears in a Babylonian document as 'Tattannu,' the governor of Beyond the River in 502 B.C. From Babylonian documents it seems a certain Ustanu was governor of Babylon and Beyond the River from March 521 until June/July 516 B.C. Ustanu was apparently satrap of this region in 520 B.C. and Tattenai probably served under him as governor for the western part of the satrapy. The investigation here in Ezra 5 took place in 520 B.C. and the Babylonian reference to Tattannu was from 502 B.C., so he must have served some twenty years at least. See, e.g., Andrew E. Steinmann, *Ezra and Nehemiah*, CC (St. Louis: Concordia, 2010), 253. Verse 4 is a bit tricky, whether the subject is 'we' or 'they.' Clearly, the ones inquiring after names were Tattenai and co., as verse 10 makes clear.

4. Such communication would not be long and drawn out (as has already been noted). Alfred Hoerth in his *Archaeology and the Old Testament* (Grand Rapids: Baker, 1998) provides more fascinating background: 'Some Bible readers may assume the people in Jerusalem waited and worried for many months, even years for the reply, but that is not the case. Darius the Great introduced several changes in the way the empire was administered, and the highway system was one of his high priorities. The Persian Royal Road stretched some seventeen hundred miles from Susa through Arbela (near Nineveh) to Sardis .... The road was carefully maintained, and rough stretches were paved. It was the Persians who invented horseshoes to facilitate mail moving over this Royal Road. Post stations were positioned on average every fifteen miles so Persian couriers could mount fresh horses. This communication network functioned so well that a letter written in Susa would reach Sardis in one week' (p. 393). Hoerth notes that a courier could average 240 miles per day and a caravan nineteen; hence if Darius' system was fully functioning at this time, the report and response would be complete in a month or two at most.

So what do we mean by a 'negative' providence? Just what 5:5 indicates: 'But the eye of their God was upon the elders of the Jews, and they did not stop them until the report should get to Darius and then the letter be returned about it.' That was not massive, but it was welcome. They could go on building while the inquiry was made. It's a *negative* providence because it deals with what God did *not* allow to happen. We do not think enough of this.

This theme is the burden of Psalm 124:

> Unless it had been Yahweh
>   who was on our side
> – let Israel now say,
> Unless it had been Yahweh
>   who was on our side
>   when men rose up against us
> – then they would have swallowed us alive,
>   when their anger burned against us;
> then the waters would have washed us away.... (vv. 1-4a)

This consideration leads to a 'benediction' on Yahweh: 'Blessed be Yahweh, who has not given us as prey to their teeth' (v. 6). The psalm seems to say: we have teeth marks but are not swallowed; we are dripping wet but not washed away; we may not sing the Hallelujah Chorus but only 'Unless the Lord had been on our side.'

George Wishart (1513–1546) eventually paid with his life at the hands of Cardinal Beaton, but he had also enjoyed 'negative' providences. Once he had received a letter, apparently from a close friend, who had become dangerously ill and wished to see Wishart before he died. (The letter was actually a forgery by the Cardinal.) Wishart set out with a few friends but had not gone more than a quarter-mile when he abruptly stopped and strangely announced, 'I am forbidden by God to go this journey; will some of you be pleased to ride to yonder place [a little hill], and see what you find, for I apprehend there is a plot laid against my life.' His friends reconnoitered and discovered some sixty horsemen, concealed, and ready to seize Wishart.[5]

---

5. Thomas M'Crie, *The Story of the Scottish Church* (Glasgow: Free Presbyterian Church, n.d.), 19-20.

Just one of the massive instances of what God does *not* allow to happen. Knees should bend and heads bow at the memory of negative providences.

Our text also suggests that the Jews enjoyed a *promiscuous* providence (5:6–6:12, especially 6:8-10), that is, a providence that was likely far more than they expected.

We can trace the text: first, there was the report and inquiry from Tattenai and associates to the central government (5:6-17); next, a search in the archives (6:1-2) came up with the discovery of the needed Cyrus document (6:3-5), validating and authorizing the temple repair project; all of which led to orders for non-interference and granting the returnees freedom to press on with construction (6:6-7). What a boon that inter-library loan from Ecbatana proved to be![6]

But then, there's more. Verse 8 begins with 'Moreover …' (ESV; literally, 'And …'), which introduces a decree Darius himself makes (6:8-12) in addition to Cyrus' re-discovered decree. He orders that the cost of re-building is to be paid from provincial resources (v. 8), that all supplies needed for sacrificial worship be provided by the same (vv. 9-10), and that dire disaster would descend on anyone daring to change such instructions (vv. 11-12).[7] But this from Darius is 'above and beyond' Cyrus' decree. This is likely more than the Jews expected. Here is financial and liturgical provision over and above. Which is why I call it promiscuous providence.

---

6. Ecbatana was the ancient capital of Media, located about 180 miles WSW of present-day Tehran. Cyrus and other Persian kings used to spend two months of summers there each year because of the relative coolness of its climate at such a time (ISBE, 2:10-11). Roland de Vaux drew a telling inference from this Ecbatana reference. We know, he said, that (1) Persian kings liked to spend summers in Susa or Ecbatana; (2) we know that Cyrus left Babylon in the spring of 538 B.C., still the 'first year' (6:3) of his reign; and so (3) the decree (= 6:3-5) must have been issued from either Susa or Ecbatana (the latter, according to 6:2). If, as sometimes radical critics love to assert, the decree was the work of a much later forger, how could such a miscreant have conjured up such an accurate detail (like the document having been found at Ecbatana)? (Roland de Vaux, 'The Decrees of Cyrus and Darius on the Rebuilding of the Temple,' in *The Bible and the Ancient Near East* [Garden City, NY: Doubleday, 1971], 89).

7. There are plenty of samples of Persian kings restoring sanctuaries throughout the empire; see Yamauchi, EBC, 4:427, for such. Darius' desire that the Jerusalem cult 'pray for the life of the king and his sons' (6:10) fits with Jeremiah's instructions to the exiles to pray for the welfare of their captors' regime (Jer. 29:7; cf. 1 Tim. 2:1-2).

It is 'vintage Yahweh.' One can't demand that Yahweh act this way, but the God of the Bible has 'tendencies,' and one tendency is to do far more than we ask or think (cf. Eph. 3:20). Somehow he is not satisfied with a *bare* providence but insists on doing more. It's as if he regards some benefit as too trivial ('too light a thing,' Isa. 49:6) and he must lavish far more. So Ezra 6 is like Exodus 2:1-10, when Moses' mother not only gets her baby back but has him under state protection with a regular government check for childcare. God tends to overflow.

It reminds me of my junior year in college: I needed a car because of a weekly preaching commitment forty miles from campus. My brother, who was connected with the Chrysler network, found me a used Dodge that looked reasonably reliable. But before I left to go back to college, 1,200 miles away, he gave me one of his credit cards. Not for normal use, but, as he said, I might have sudden car repairs or expenses and not have enough to cover the cost. In such cases, I was to use his credit card. It was an 'over and above' provision. And that was God's way here in Jerusalem: the Jews received far more than mere permission to rebuild, simply because Yahweh's providence has a tendency to extravagance.

Then this providence is also a *hidden* providence. Most English versions translate the summary note in 6:14 as: 'they finished building according to the command of the God of Israel and the decree of Cyrus, Darius, and Artaxerxes king of Persia.'[8] But 'command' is really the word 'decree.' The ESV has nicely picked this up: 'they finished their building by decree of the God of Israel and by the decree of Cyrus,' etc. There is the Lord's decree, and there is the decree of Persian kings. The ultimate decree is God's; but he clothes his decree in the decrees of kings and men and hides or covers his way in this indirect manner. Nevertheless, it is clear that in their decrees and pronouncements, kings are only the servant-boys of the most high God.

---

8. What is Artaxerxes doing here since he comes after (464–423 b.c.) the temple re-building? I'm not sure, but *if* Ezra was the one responsible for compiling chapters 1–6, he may have tacked on Artaxerxes because that king had also showed Ezra favor by authorizing his ministry in Judah (7:1ff.); cf. Robert Fyall, *The Message of Ezra and Haggai*, BST (Downers Grove, IL: Inter-Varsity, 2010), 92.

So it happened. Renewed work on the temple had begun on 21 September 520 B.C. (Hag. 1:14-15) and finished in the last Babylonian month, Adar (February–March), on 12 March 515 B.C., roughly seventy years after it had been destroyed.[9]

So far, I've indicated that both prophecy and providence got the exiles off of 'dead center' to finish the building of the temple. The last section of text focuses on their response when the project was finished. Here I think the Jews would say **joy carries us** (6:16-22). This section consists of two parts, 6:16-18, the last of the current Aramaic portion, and 6:19-22, where the text swings back to Hebrew. Notice, however, the stress on joy at the beginning and at the end of the whole section: they 'celebrated the dedication of this house of God with joy' (v. 16), and they 'carried out the feast of Unleavened Bread seven days with joy, for Yahweh had made them joyful' (v. 22). If we milk this context, we might discover what fed this joy.

First, there was joy over *restored worship* (vv. 16-18). The sacrifices at the dedication were not as lavish as those in Solomon's (1 Kings 8:5, 63), Hezekiah's (2 Chron. 30:24), and Josiah's (2 Chron. 35:7) celebrations, but the offerings (v. 17) and personnel (v. 18) were functioning again in orthodox fashion in line with Moses' prescriptions.

Then, one could say they were joyful over *remembered redemption* (vv. 19-20). Come the first month, they are eager for Passover, when (they could recall) Israel was kept free from Yahweh's wrath by the blood of the lamb (Exod. 12:12-13) and set free from bondage to Egypt. Here in Ezra 6, there is such a diligence and eagerness about the ceremonial preparation of the priests and Levites; they were not slovenly or indifferent about this opportunity. And perhaps this post-exilic community looked upon this Passover as commemorating a 'second exodus,' i.e., from exile in Babylon. If verses 16-18 show a restored people, verses 19-20 remember a redeemed people.

Isn't there also a hint of joy over *converted people* (v. 21)? Notice the 'and also' in this verse. It wasn't only the returned exiles who ate this Passover but 'all who had joined them and

---

9. Yamauchi, EBC, 4:429.

separated themselves from the pollutions of the nations of the land' (NRSV) to worship Yahweh. Who were these folks? Probably some were lapsed Jews who'd remained in the land and had melted into syncretistic religion; and probably some gentile converts who had been attracted to the new Jerusalem community.[10] Here were conversions. And this note (here in v. 21) should correct a mis-impression sometimes taken from 4:3. Chapter 4, verse 3, was not narrow-minded nationalism; 6:21 must be placed beside it. Here (6:21) is a community open to others; yet there is a price to pay – they must 'separate themselves' from the impurity of the nations. The church does not win the world by becoming like the world; it must insist that the world leave the world when it enters the church. But this text shows that the post-exilic 'church' was not some closed-door group of bigoted, gentile-despising Jews. However, the way into this body was not through some loose-as-a-goose pagan ecumenism (4:1-3), but through costly and decisive conversion. And that should be a matter for joy.

Finally, verse 22 implies these Jews were joyful over *delightful providence.* We're told they observed Unleavened Bread (following Passover) 'with joy, for Yahweh had made them joyful.' Then in the next breath the writer adds: 'and [Yahweh] had turned round the heart of the king of Assyria' to encourage them in their temple project.[11] It seems to be the writer's rather strange way of referring to King Darius and Yahweh's secret, silent way of moving an earthly king to carry out the heavenly King's will. Another matter for joy.

---

10. cf. D. J. A. Clines, *Ezra, Nehemiah, Esther,* NCBC (Grand Rapids: Eerdmans, 1984), 97.

11. Why would Darius, the king of Persia, be dubbed the 'king of Assyria' here? F. C. Fensham's comment may not be the last word on the matter but is, I think, a useful one: 'We have evidence from the ancient Near East that new rulers or foreign rulers were incorporated in the king lists of a particular country. This is the case with a king list of Babylon, which starts with the Assyrian Kandalanu, mentions the Chaldeans Nabopolassar and Nebuchadnezzar, refers to Cyrus, Cambyses, and Darius, and ends with the names of Seleucid kings. Because Darius was also the sovereign of Assyria, he could easily have been called king of Assyria. The choice of this title might seem awkward. It is possible that the author wanted to refer here to a title which had for a long time in history inspired fear in the hearts of the Jews. The Assyrian kings were used by the Lord to chastise his people (cf. Neh. 9:32). But now the Lord had used the Assyrian king (Darius) to grant favor to the Jews, a great change in the historical situation' (*The Books of Ezra and Nehemiah,* NICOT [Grand Rapids: Eerdmans, 1982], 96-97).

Such joy, however, is not locked up in 520 B.C. with post-exilic Israelite worshipers. 'Yahweh made them joyful' can often be written of his people even in their rather ordinary circumstances. The text reminds one of Franz Josef Haydn's response when his exuberant music was criticized by some more somber members of the church: 'Since God has given me a cheerful heart, He will forgive me for serving Him cheerfully.' Once when Haydn was setting to music the words of the Mass (in Anglo: 'Lamb of God, who takes away the sins of the world'), he says that he was seized by an 'uncontrollable gladness.' He even had to apologize to the Empress Marie Therese on the matter; he explained that the certainty of God's grace had made him so happy that he wrote a joyful melody for the sober words.[12] Thankfully God often tends to do that – to give us a joy that carries us.

---

12. Patrick Kavanaugh, *The Spiritual Lives of the Great Composers* (Nashville: Sparrow, 1992), 21-22.

6

Torah Comes to Town
(Ezra 7)

I was a new and young pastor, trying to make pastoral calls on my small town and rural flock. One afternoon I knocked at a door and discovered I should have gone to the house next door. But this door was answered by an elderly man named Smith, who insisted I come in and visit anyway. He was a retired lawyer, and loquacious. In the course of conversation he alluded to a minister he knew. Smith had suggested this minister should preach from the words in Hosea 2:15, 'And make the Valley of Achor [trouble] a door of hope.' 'Oh, Smith,' said the minister, 'that's too big! That's too big!' Apparently he thought the text was so loaded he could not get his mind around it nor dare to draw a sermon from it. Analogically, that's the way I feel about Ezra 7–8. The 'hand' of God is the theme that pervades these chapters (7:6, 9, 28; 8:18, 22, 31), but taking both chapters together simply encompasses so much material that I'm forced with Smith's friend to exclaim, 'That's too big!' Hence I feel compelled to break it up and begin by treating chapter 7 by itself, which focuses on the coming of Ezra in 458 B.C.[1]

We should notice, first, **the place God's servant occupies** (vv. 1-6).

---

1. This dating is fairly generally acknowledged now. I think it is correct. I know there are those who argue, via various considerations, for 428 or 398 B.C. I waded through the whole issue in graduate school and have no desire to spit it all out again. Readers who are dying to investigate the matter can consult the larger commentaries or histories of Israel.

We begin by noting Ezra's place *in the book*. Verse 1 begins with its non-threatening 'And after these things.' That is, the 'things' of chapters 1–6. After six chapters, we finally meet up with Ezra. However, there is a gap of around sixty years between the matters at the end of chapter 6 and those of chapter 7 – which tells us how *selective* our writer/editor is. He does not intend to provide a running, detailed report of post-exilic life in Judah; rather, he highlights key moments in that period. He had highlighted their *restored worship* in chapters 1–6, and now he will speak of their *reformed life* in chapters 7–10, life in accord with the torah of God. Our writer will not tell us of all things but only of what he deems significant things – and that means he can skip sixty years if he wants to do so. So ... Ezra shows up two-thirds of the way through the book that bears his name.

The immediate text, however, underscores Ezra's place *in history*, which we can see from the genealogy in verses 1-5. The genealogy provides credentials for Ezra – it authenticates Ezra's place and identity, a crucial matter in that context (remember 2:59-63).[2] One couldn't claim a hearing just because he had a website and a blog! The genealogy with its sixteen steps traces Ezra back to Aaron, the first high priest of Israel. The genealogy has omissions or gaps. We know this because of the fuller (twenty-three step) genealogy of high priests in 1 Chronicles 6:3-15, but even that genealogy has 'gaps.'[3] This is not unusual in biblical genealogies. But there is enough genetic linkage here to establish Ezra as a bona fide, card-carrying priest.

Derek Thomas reminds us that though we may stifle a yawn at such a genealogy,

> to Ezra's initial audience, it was like a fanfare of trumpets signaling his importance. Someone special had arrived. He burst onto the scene waving credentials that showed him to be of the most significant genetic line in Israel – the line of Aaron.[4]

---

2. See Derek W. H. Thomas, *Ezra & Nehemiah*, REC (Phillipsburg, NJ: P & R, 2016), 114.

3. See Martin J. Selman, *1 Chronicles*, TOTC (Downers Grove, IL: Inter-Varsity, 1994), 108-9.

4. Thomas, 114. See Also Mervin Breneman, *Ezra, Nehemiah, Esther*, NAC (n. p: Broadman & Holman, 1993), 126 (drawing on Eskenazi).

Yet this genealogy shows that Ezra (the 'end term') stands in a *history* of God's servants (and of a few rogues as well). There have been many before him. It is always well for us to remember this. God has had a history with his people, caring for them, preserving them through various servants before Ezra – or we – ever showed up. Much has happened before our time. This should keep us from that creeping arrogance that thinks we have the latest skill-set for a moribund church.

I remember a few years ago when I was writing a commentary on the Book of Judges, that I was quite pleased to observe a parallel and repeating literary pattern in Judges 10:6-16 and 11:1-11. But then I discovered that in about 1708 Matthew Henry had already noted the same pattern. Always helpful and humbling to realize that God has had other servants who have fruitfully labored over his word before we ever came along. Jesus sums it up nicely in John 4:38b: 'Others have labored, and you have entered into their labor.'

Then too, don't miss Ezra's place *in providence* (v. 6). This verse describes Ezra as a 'skilled' (*mahir*) scribe in the torah of Moses, a torah that was Yahweh's gift to Israel. The root behind 'skilled' suggests 'speedy' or 'quick.' The idea is likely that Ezra was speedy in his work because he was so skilled. He was super-competent, or, as NJPS has it, 'a scribe expert in the Teaching of Moses.' But note especially the latter part of verse 6:

> And the king gave him,
> according to the hand of Yahweh his God upon him,
> all that he asked.

This implies that what Artaxerxes decreed in verses 12-26 was in response to Ezra's request. And the king's favorable answer was because of the 'hand of Yahweh' upon Ezra. This is the first of those 'hand' of God/Yahweh notes in chapters 7–8. Note the combination: human initiative (what Ezra asked) and divine providence (the hand of Yahweh) are compatible bedfellows. They work nicely together. Ezra apparently didn't sit around stewing over whether what he had in mind was 'God's will.' He laid his requests before the king and found that the hand of Yahweh was at work in, around, and under his request. It's really the same sort of 'animal' as one sees in Jonathan's faith in 1 Samuel 14:6: 'Come on, and let's cross over to the garrison of these uncircumcised fellows; perhaps Yahweh will act for us, for nothing can keep Yahweh from saving by many or by few.' Who knows what Yahweh may take pleasure in doing? Ezra must have believed the same theology. Divine providence and/or divine sovereignty does not stifle human initiative – it invites it. And so here Ezra has the delight of wallowing in the providence of God.

Secondly, the text emphasizes **the purpose God's servant fulfills** (vv. 7-10, with emphasis on v. 10). A various entourage travels with Ezra to Jerusalem in the seventh year of (I believe) Artaxerxes I. The trip from Babylon to Jerusalem was 500 miles for a crow but 900 for Ezra and co. since they would follow the northward bend of the Euphrates. So, by those who can calculate, the journey took four months, from early April to early August, 458 B.C.[5] The safe journey was 'in line with the good hand of his God upon him' (v. 9). The writer cannot keep from injecting praise even in the details of a travelogue. And apparently God's hand was upon Ezra precisely because of his determined purpose (v. 10; note the 'For' in 10a).

Let us look more closely at verse 10:

> For Ezra had set his heart to seek the torah of Yahweh, and to do (it), and to teach in Israel statutes and rules.[6]

The language of this verse speaks of a ministry that is *focused in its objective* ('set his heart') and *intense in its labor* (to seek torah). It is both *anchored* and *vigorous*. Ezra was not going to be content with a little ministerial piddling. And note how Ezra purposes a total ministry: here the infinitives are telling – to seek, to do, to teach. The first involves, if not entirely at least substantially, a *cognitive* element; the

---

5. See Yamauchi, EBC, 4:434.

6. I use 'torah' – it is usually translated as 'law,' but it is much broader than what we conceive as law. 'Torah' is equivalent to teaching, instruction, or doctrine. Law may be part of it, but torah is broader than 'law.' Andrew Steinmann notes that Ezra 7:10 is the only place in the OT where the object of 'seek' (i.e., Heb. *darash*) is 'torah' (*Ezra and Nehemiah*, CC [St. Louis: Concordia, 2010], 289). For a fine sermon on Ezra 7:10, rummage through back issues of 'Christianity Today' (Nov. 23, 1962), 5-7, for Alec Motyer's exposition.

next, 'to do,' is *experiential*, and the last 'teach' deals with the *didactic*.[7]

Clearly, the order of these activities is crucial. To seek torah implies a total familiarity with biblical revelation. But this is not for accumulating a mere theological database. Rather it is in order 'to do' it, to incorporate that word in the obedience of one's own life. And then, only in the wake of the seeking and the doing is one qualified 'to teach' in Israel the details of torah. The program – to seek, to do, to teach – then, moves from *concentration* (mind-saturated) to *consistency* (life-conformed) to *communication* (ministry-driven). In that order.

I've always been haunted by that story Richard Bewes told of speaking with an atheist who taught theology in a UK university. 'So why theology?' Richard asked him. 'It amuses me' was his reply. One would never get such a damnably casual response from Ezra! He was a beaver for torah and for living it out and for rubbing it into the pores of God's people. Ezra 7:10 depicts a model servant and a proper 'philosophy of ministry.'

Finally, notice **the politics God's servant enjoys** (vv. 11-28). The text contains a copy of the letter or decree Artaxerxes gave Ezra, authorizing his mission; it is spread out in full in verses 13-26. One is tempted to speculate. Some have suggested that Ezra may have had a position in the Persian bureaucracy, something like 'Secretary of State for Jewish Affairs.'[8] It might not be too wild to imagine the king telling Ezra to ghost-write the decree, and, if the draft met his approval, he would 'sign off' on it. We simply don't know; but we do know there were two primary provisions in the decree.

First, it gave *royal approval for a torah-mission* (vv. 14, 25-26). The usual translation of verse 14 says that the Persian administration authorized Ezra 'to make inquiries about Judah and Jerusalem.' It sounds like Ezra is on a fact-finding mission. However, Steinmann (drawing on Richard Steiner's work) contends that the use of the Aramaic *beqar* here with the

---

7. This cognitive element shows there is an *academic* component in the ministry of the word, but the intensity implied in the verb 'to seek,' indicates it is a *hungry* academic component. It is never a *merely* academic affair.

8. See discussion in D. J. A. Clines, *Ezra, Nehemiah, Esther*, NCBC (Grand Rapids: Eerdmans, 1984), 99.

preposition *'al* means 'to exercise the office of overseer over' people. So Steinmann translates, 'to be superintendent over Yehud [Judah] and Jerusalem.'[9] In short, Ezra has a far more authoritative role than gathering information and assessing current conditions. Verses 25-26 support this view. There Ezra is authorized to appoint magistrates and judges to order life in line with 'the law of your God and the law of the king' (v. 26) and to impose punishments for non-compliance, even up to the death penalty. Ezra is no paper figurehead.[10] His authority in 'Beyond the River' is likely restricted to Jews (v. 25b), but any number of those Jews may've lived outside of Judah/Jerusalem.[11] His commission involved a commitment to teaching 'the laws of your God.'[12] Torah had come to town!

The second element in the royal decree authorizes *abundant provision for ongoing worship* (vv. 15-20, 21-23). Both the silver and the gold given by the government (v. 15) and that raised at large (v. 16) was to be used to purchase sacrificial animals and supplies for worship at the Jerusalem temple (v. 17). Then the provincial treasury was to kick in supplies as well (vv. 21-22).[13] Temple functionaries were to have a 'clergy exemption' from taxation (v. 24). In any case, there was to be full-orbed temple worship in Jerusalem – in the government's view as a propitiatory protection for the king and his sons (v. 23b).[14]

---

9. Steinmann, 293.

10. 'Significantly, Ezra had the power of imposing the death penalty upon those guilty of capital crimes (e.g., idolatry [Exod. xxii 20; Lev. xx 2ff.; Deut. xiii 6-10] or adultery [Lev. xx 10; Deut. xxii 22]), whether against the law of God or the law of the king. This simply means that Ezra had behind him the authority of the Persian government' (Jacob M. Myers, *Ezra, Nehemiah*, AB [Garden City, NY: Doubleday, 1965], 62-63).

11. But see Yamauchi, EBC, 4:439, citing M. Heltzer's view of an expanded authority.

12. One assumes then that Ezra's administrative and didactic duties would entail a significant amount of travel; he hardly ensconced himself in a bureaucratic office in Jerusalem.

13. Edwin Yamauchi (EBC, 4:438) supplies equivalents for amounts in verse 22: A talent weighed about 75 pounds, so 100 talents of silver was an enormous amount, nearly three-quarters of a ton; a 'cor' was a donkey load, about six and a half bushels. The total amount of wheat was 650 bushels. A bath was a liquid measure of about six gallons, so the oil came to 600 gallons. Some of these supplies would run out – perhaps some were 'starter' amounts.

14. Moreover, '[s]upport for a community's cult(s) was a sure way to gain its loyalty, and the Persian emperors were quick off the mark to secure their rule

Verses 27-28 are a first-person clip from Ezra himself. He erupts in praise over his delight in Persian politics brought about by Yahweh. He underscores what we might call the subtle sovereignty of Yahweh, 'who has placed something like this in the heart of the king' (v. 27). King Artaxerxes may make the decree and grant the permission, but *why* does he do so? Because there is a King behind the king, One who turns the king's heart whichever way he wants (Prov. 21:1). Yahweh's sovereignty, however, is not always blatant and dramatic; frequently, as here, it is hidden and subtle.[15]

This seeming 'ordinariness' of God's sovereignty should not be a problem for us. Why should we always expect the dramatic and rambunctious? When Thomas Jefferson was president he was willing to receive unscheduled visitors during the day, though he never felt obliged to get 'spruced up' for such occasions. So once, in 1802, Senator Plumer with Congressman Varnum came to meet Jefferson. A tall, high-boned man entered the room. Plumer said that he 'was dressed, or rather undressed, in an old brown coat, red waistcoat, old corduroy small-clothes much-soiled, woolen hose, and slippers without heels.'[16] Plumer thought he was a servant but his friend 'surprised me by announcing that it was the President.' One could choose to be 'offended' by such commonness, but this is often the wrapper Yahweh uses for his sovereignty. It's there in what seems such ordinariness – unless, like Ezra, we can detect it by faith and delight in it by worship.

---

over the vast domains they inherited from Babylon and Media by this means' (K. A. Kitchen, *On the Reliability of the Old Testament* [Grand Rapids: Eerdmans, 2003], 76).

15. We meet the same in verse 28. There the words 'upon me' are emphatic. As if Ezra exclaims, 'Imagine! Even on *me* Yahweh showed *hesed* (kindness) before the king and his advisors.' But it was all so low-key and 'normal' – in the process of the interviews and making his requests he saw that Yahweh had prospered him.

16. Ian W. Toll, *Six Frigates* (New York: W. W. Norton, 2006), 266.

7

Jerusalem – or Bust
(Ezra 8)

Late last summer my wife and I drove 3,600 miles on a trip through the US Great Plains and back home. Barbara even assembled an album with pictures and brief comments about our various stops. So, we'll remember the Pancake House in Liberal, Kansas, what Valentine, Nebraska, looked like, the capital grounds in Pierre, South Dakota, and the motel where we stayed when our vehicle broke down on an interstate in Indiana. She did a superb piece of work. But, as a rule, biblical journeys are passed over in silence. Note verses 31-32. Merely a bare notice. Nothing about where favorite restaurants were, or, in their case, the most luxurious caravan oases. One meets the 'hand of our God' theme again in chapter 8 (vv. 18, 22, 31), not least in reference to the safety of the journey; here the objects of the 'hand of God' are plural, while in chapter 7 (vv. 6, 9, 28) they were all singular (Ezra). But, as verses 31-32 imply, no need to bother about details. Only gratitude to God and arrival in Jerusalem. That's all that matters.

If the trip itself receives scant attention, chapter 8 nevertheless gives a good bit of space to those who returned, to necessary preparations for the journey, to the goods that they transported, and to the first order of business upon arrival. So we should give our attention to these highlights.

Notice, first, how the text depicts **the congregation of God** (vv. 1-14). And right at the start it contains *a flicker of hope* (vv. 2-3a). Descendants of two priestly lines are noted and then a descendant 'from the sons of David, Hattush from the sons of Shecaniah' (cf. NIV). No bells ringing, but there is Hattush.

We can go back to the listing of the Davidic descendants in 1 Chronicles 3:17-24. I know there are some difficulties about how to construe the details of that text. But if one scrutinizes that list carefully, it seems, as Fensham says, that the main thread of the list is: Jehoiachin, Pedaiah, Zerubbabel, Hananiah, Shecaniah, Shemaiah, Hattush. 'Thus Hattush is the fourth generation after Zerubbabel. If Zerubbabel was born c. 560 B.C. and if we reckon approximately twenty-five years for a generation, the date for Hattush comes close to 458 B.C.'[1]

The writer, however, does not go ballistic over the presence of a Davidic descendant here. The emphasis is muted.[2] But he does mention him. Perhaps we can imagine a scenario from something like a Louis L'Amour western. Thugs and ruffians have carried off a young lady to hold her for ransom. The hero of our story pursues, trying to pick up their trail. Then he comes upon a piece of red scarf, a scarf he knows belongs to the girl. It is caught, seemingly by accident, on a mesquite shrub. But he divines she deliberately snagged it there so her rescuer would know she had been this way – and to encourage him to pursue. The scarf is not the girl but simply a sign that she is apparently alive and that our hero is on the right path. Perhaps Hattush fulfills that role here. He's a sign that, even in the drab days of these post-exilic years, the line of David is still intact. Is the mention of Hattush, a 'son' of David, meant as a hint that the Davidic covenant, though currently eclipsed, is not dead and buried, that God has not repealed the promise of 2 Samuel 7?

There's more here: verses 3-14 testify to what we might call *a place for genetics*. Those who came back with Ezra tended to be from those families that had come back c. 538 B.C., eighty years before (see Ezra 2). Note the links in the following listing:

---

1. F. C. Fensham, *The Books of Ezra and Nehemiah*, NICOT (Grand Rapids: Eerdmans, 1982), 111.

2. See J. G. McConville, *Ezra, Nehemiah, and Esther*, Daily Study Bible (Philadelphia: Westminster, 1985), 54.

8:3	Parosh	2:3
8:4	Pahath-moab	2:6
8:5	Zattu	2:8
8:6	Adin	2:15
8:7	Elam	2:7
8:8	Shephatiah	2:4
8:9	Joab	
8:10	Bani	2:10
8:11	Bebai	2:11
8:12	Azgad	2:12
8:13	Adonikam	2:13
8:14	Bigvai	2:14

The overall message here seems to be: Don't trust in genetics (Matthew 3:9 is true) but *don't despise genetics* – after all, covenant fidelity tends to run in families.

> Even over the generations, it was particular families that were to the fore in making the journey back to the land. Reading between the lines, we may discern here an example of that faith-in-action ... transmitted from generation to generation by whole families which took seriously their religious and educative duties.[3]

This should be a word of hope to godly fathers and mothers today. Doesn't this a-place-for-genetics point help to answer the question: What can I do for the kingdom of God? Answer: Indoctrinate your kids, lead a godly life among them, and love and pray that they will claim the faith for themselves. Is that a sure-fire guarantee? No, it is not. But ... largely the reason I am in the kingdom of God today is that my father and mother taught me a kingdom gospel and lived a kingdom life before me.

The Bible is nothing but candid. The second highlight of the text has to do with **the drudgery of service** (vv. 15-20). Anxiety at Ahava. No Levites. So Ezra sends a committee (v. 16) to Casiphia (v. 17).[4] Who knows where that was? Apparently, it was a site near Babylon – perhaps a Jewish

---

3. McConville, 53.

4. No need to have a paroxysm over the three Elnathans among Ezra's ambassadors. Probably no more unusual than three 'Georges' would be for us.

study center? In any case, headmaster Iddo must have persuaded Sherebiah and his cohorts and Hashabiah and Jeshaiah with theirs to consider a Jerusalem ministry. Net total, 38 Levites. And 220 temple servants (vv. 18-20). Hardly an overwhelming response but still evidence of 'the good hand of our God' (v. 18a).

What do we make of this? Well, there was likely a level of comfort, even prosperity, for the exiles in Babylon. But if Levites, for example, go with Ezra back to Judea, they will leave a life where they have a good deal of autonomy for the 'strict routines of the temple' (Kidner), in Judea, where life was not all fulfillment and fun. Doing temple guard duty or assisting priests with the messy process of sacrifice may have been less than alluring. And temple servants likely did not salivate over custodial duty of cleaning up temple gunk.

Years ago there was a clip in 'Leadership' magazine about how a Chicago bank asked for a letter of recommendation for a young Bostonian being considered for employment. The Boston investment house exuded over the young man. His father was a Cabot, his mother a Lowell. Further back there was a marvelous blend of Saltonstalls, Peabodys, and others of Boston's elite. He was recommended heartily. Several days later, the Chicago bank sent a note notifying the investment operation that the information given was completely inadequate. It stated: 'We are not contemplating using the young man for breeding purposes. Just for work.'

Just for work. But that was just the problem in Jerusalem. And the fewer Levites meant all the more work. The prospect was scarcely glamorous. And yet they came.

All this may carry a word of correction for the western church today. Sometimes we need to remember that not all of Christ's work is exciting and is not intended to enhance our self-esteem. We naturally desire a calling that operates in semi-appealing circumstances. But what if, as Eugene Peterson imagines, we find ourselves 'in a town of three thousand people on the far edge of Kansas, in which the library is underbudgeted, the radio station plays only country music, the high school football team provides all the celebrities that town can manage, and a covered-dish supper is the high-point of congregational life'?[5] Not all of Christ's service drips with 'fulfillment.' So here were Levites and temple servants trudging to Jerusalem. My hunch is that they did it because they thought Yahweh would want them to do so.

Thirdly, Ezra's report underscores **the risk of theology** (vv. 21-23, 31-32). We can summarize the matter like this: Ezra and co.'s profession of faith (v. 22b) presses them to the proving of faith (v. 22a), all of which is supported by their prayers of faith (vv. 21, 23) to which God granted the vindication of faith (vv. 23b, 31).

You can sense the rub. Ezra *et al.* had told Artaxerxes that 'the hand of our God is upon all who seek him for good, but his power and wrath are against all who forsake him' (v. 22b). If that's the case, why should their caravan need an escort of Persian soldiers (v. 22a)? If we have the hand of God, why do we need the troops of Persia? This is the risk of faith. Ezra probably believed there are times when faith must take on flesh, when what is professed must be lived out, expressed in concrete situations. So they engage in fasting and prayer, seeking a safe journey (v. 21). This pleading and confession does not contradict their professed confidence but is an expression of it.

Here was no trivial undertaking. It was a 900-mile journey. There were over 1,500 men (vv. 1-14) with families and children (note v. 21, 'our little ones'), and likely servants – so at least a body of 5,000. If word was out about the x-amount of goods they were transporting, their caravan would prove tantalizing to – as the KJV might say, 'men of the baser sort.' Ezra must have been a superb administrator, but there was danger written all over this journey.

Such travel at that time was precarious – the usual hazards included water shortage, adverse weather, wild beasts, and marauding bandits. Even the Persian 'Royal Road' did not eliminate such threats. Progress might be 18–20 miles/day.[6]

---

5. Eugene H. Peterson, *Under the Unpredictable Plant* (Grand Rapids: Eerdmans, 1992), 129. I myself would find the far edge of Kansas rather appealing, but then mine is probably a minority opinion.

6. Readers may find it instructive to check Barry J. Beitzel, 'Travel and Communication,' ABD, 6:644-47.

And in all this Ezra and his friends were looking to 'the good hand of our God' for protection.[7]

Ezra's situation and decision should prove useful for us. It shows that there are times when faith gets pushed beyond the theoretical, times when faith must be tested. But in facing such matters and in making such choices (as Ezra had to do here), how do we discern the difference between faith and folly? Am I believing God by not taking a military escort or am I simply being stupid? How do I know? Am I tempting God or trusting God? And how can I tell the difference? Or look at it from the other angle: if Ezra took an escort, would he then be acting in prudence or in unbelief? Many of us have faced such conundrums, and often there is no easy answer. But the point still remains: if we have a theology like verse 22b, time will come when we must risk living it.

Our chapter closes by stressing **the urgency of integrity** (vv. 24-30, 33-34). Ezra set up an oversight committee to have charge of and to guard the substantial wealth from government and personal sources they were transporting (v. 24).[8] Some scholars swallow hard over the tallies of these gifts (vv. 26-27): 650 talents of silver would be about twenty-four tons, 100 gold talents over three tons. Isn't it too massive? Were the numerals passed on accurately? But both the Persian government and many Jews in Babylon were filthy rich, so, unless we get more light on the matter, we should accept the text as it is. Just make sure there's a horde of donkeys to carry the stuff.

Ezra then reports the tallies involved (vv. 24-27), the vigilance demanded (vv. 28-30), and the transfer accomplished (vv. 33-34). The arduous journey is passed over in silence ('so we came to Jerusalem,' v. 32), but the weighing out and delivery of their 'cargo' to Meremoth and

---

7. Because Ezra declined an escort by Persian troops does not mean that this caravan took no measures for defense. These Jews were hardly a bunch of committed pacifists. And numbers of them surely went armed, if only to fend off wild animals – or potential brigands.

8. On verse 24, cf. e.g., Brian Aucher, 'Ezra–Nehemiah,' *ESV Expository Commentary*, 12 vols. (Wheaton, IL: Crossway, 2020), 4:95. The committee likely consisted of twelve priests and twelve Levites.

associates is clearly and carefully recorded (vv. 33-34). It's as if Ezra is obsessed with the careful guarding and faithful transfer of this wealth. Doesn't this reflect Ezra's concern to make integrity obvious? He has such a passion for honesty, such a fixation on total transparency in these dealings. He wants to ensure no one can accuse him of hidden deals or siphoned funds. No one must have any reason for suspicion. Because the king has highly privileged you does not mean that you ignore more mundane matters.

Paul showed the same obsession for demonstrable honesty when he was organizing the Judea Relief Collection. He was soliciting funds from the Corinthian church and others for needy believers in Israel. He made sure there were others appointed with oversight of this gift – he wanted no one able to accuse him of 'having his hand in the till.' Hence he wrote:

> It is a task that brings glory to God and demonstrates also the willingness of us Christians to help each other. Naturally we want to avoid the slightest breach of criticism in the distribution of their gifts, and to be absolutely above-board not only in the sight of God but in the eyes of men (2 Cor. 8:19b-21, Phillips).

This principle of public integrity has a wide application in Christian life and ministry, one that goes far beyond the particulars of Ezra's situation. We should not smile at the minister who insists there must be a large window in the office where he may be counseling or conferring with, among others, women from his congregation. And I have noted elsewhere how Dr James Baird, sometime pastor of First Presbyterian, Jackson, Mississippi, once told a group of us how the president of his seminary closed his address to the graduating class. 'Gentleman,' he said, 'pay your bills.' He had seen too many ministers who had assumed some sort of 'clergy privilege' that placed them above such routine chores – and which therefore ruined their testimony. We must let Ezra teach us: be faithful in the fiscal.

The journey of Ezra and his crowd ended where it always should – in worship (vv. 35-36). What a moving occasion it must have been: 'For these [returned] worshipers, it was the first time they had offered such an offering.'[9]

---

9. Derek W. H. Thomas, *Ezra and Nehemiah*, REC (Phillipsburg, NJ: P & R, 2016), 164.

8

Trouble in Covenant City
(Ezra 9)

In late April 1865, the Civil War between the states was all but over and Union soldiers who'd been held in southern prison camps were getting to go back to their Ohio, Indiana, and Illinois homes. At Vicksburg, Mississippi, there was a sidewheel steamer, *Sultana*, about to head up to Cairo, Illinois. Prisoners released, war over, transportation available, home beckoning, decent meals! All looked fine. But the sun stopped shining. *Sultana* was loaded with mules and troops to six times its authorized capacity and, north of Memphis, its boilers blew causing some 1,500 deaths. All seemed well, then disaster.[1] It's not as explosive here in Ezra, but the pattern is the same: things seem in good order, then all comes unglued. In chapters 7–8, the 458 B.C. contingent, the 'second wave' of returnees, comes with the blessing of the Persian government, safely arrives in Jerusalem, worships at the temple, and delivers their credentials. Then it seems to backfire: chapter 9, verses 1-2, abruptly report a major mess of covenant infidelity.

It seems abrupt. It occurs 'after these things' (v. 1), that is, after the successful journey of chapters 7–8. Actually, combining the time indicators in 7:9, 8:31, and especially

---

1. Shelby Foote, *The Civil War*, 3 vols. (New York: Random House, 1974), 3:1026-27.

10:9, it appears that these returnees had been back in Jerusalem about four and a half months when the problem of 9:1-2 was brought to Ezra's attention. Some scholars get nervous over the time delay and propose that perhaps the episode of Nehemiah 8 actually took place between Ezra 8 and 9. No need for such a knee-jerk reaction. We have to keep in mind that Ezra–Nehemiah is a *selective* document and doesn't intend to fill in all details of Ezra's activity and itinerary. Of course 8:36 hints that, after arrival, Ezra may have spent time away from Jerusalem establishing his credentials with regional officials. But we don't need to fill in all 'gaps.' All we need to know is that 'after these things' (v. 1) – even some four months after – the trouble of chapter 9 hit the fan.

The chapter breaks down into two major sections:

> The report and reaction of Ezra, vv. 1-5
> The prayer and confession of Ezra, vv. 6-15

And Ezra's prayer begins with (1) the guilt we've amassed (vv. 6-7) and moves on to (2) the grace we've enjoyed (vv. 8-9), (3) the word we've received (vv. 10-12), to end with (4) the precipice where we stand (vv. 13-15). My treatment will, to a certain extent, mix both major sections together.

What then does the text set before us? The text sets before us, first of all, **the perennial allergy of God's people** (vv. 1-2, 6-7, 10-12).

Imagine the disappointment, the blow, that the report of verses 1-2 must have been to Ezra. After the providence, preparation, prayer, and preservation of chapters 7–8 ... now this. The accusation is that 'the people of Israel have not separated themselves – this includes the priests and the Levites – from the peoples of the lands' (v. 1). The 'peoples of the lands' are the paganized or half-paganized residents surrounding the enclave of the returned exiles. The accusers go down the roster of pagan peoples from Abraham to Artaxerxes. They are not saying that 'the peoples of the lands' are Canaanites, Hittites, Perizzites, etc., but that they resemble them. Goswell rightly translates verse 1b as: '... from the peoples of the lands, *whose practices are like* the abominations of the Canaanites, the Hittites, the Perizzites' on down to the Amorites.[2] The peoples around Judah ape the practices of these historical pagans. The word 'abominations' or 'detestable practices' (*to'ebot*)

> refers to blatant idolatry and the abhorrent practices associated with it, such as child sacrifice and sexual perversions – including incest, homosexuality, and bestiality – which God deems detestable and deserving of judgment.[3]

The trouble is that the people of Israel 'have not separated themselves' (v. 1) but 'have mixed themselves' (v. 2, cf. AV) with these surrounding people groups by intermarriage, clearly violating the torah (Exod. 34:11-16; Deut. 7:1-6). This was not a racial phobia; it was a religious phobia. Practice such intermarriage and you can kiss covenant fidelity goodbye. And what is extra sad, the accusers say, is that our leaders are especially taken up in 'this treachery' (last of v. 2).

Now note the beginning of Ezra's prayer (vv. 6-7).[4] He confesses that there's such a *tedium* about all this. He speaks of their present offense (v. 6) but then says this has been an ongoing historical pattern (v. 7):

> From the days of our fathers we (have been) in immense guilt to this day, and because of our iniquities we, our kings, our priests, have been given into the hand of the kings of the lands ....

Ezra seems to say, it has always been this way; we never seem to be able to get it right; it's the same awful story over and over again. In short, what tedium! Infidelity is so *boring*. It only does re-runs. Is bondage perhaps the problem?

Yet the immediate dilemma is that the people 'have not separated themselves' (v. 1). And Ezra picks up this matter in verses 10-12 in his prayer. Israel has had the Word of God about this affair. For in these verses Ezra essentially takes us back to texts like Deuteronomy 7:1-6, where Israel is said to be a 'holy' people (v. 6), and part of being holy has to do

---

2. Gregory Goswell, *A Study Commentary on Ezra–Nehemiah* (Darlington: EP Books, 2013), 167 (emphasis mine).

3. Andrew E. Steinmann, *Ezra and Nehemiah*, CC (St. Louis: Concordia, 2010), 328.

4. Observe the pronouns in verses 6-7: 'we,' 'our.' Ezra does not place himself outside these guilty people but identifies with them.

with marriage (v. 3) because it will largely determine fidelity or apostasy (v. 4). Intermarriage with pagans will soon make Israel just another Baal-kissing, Asherah-hugging, bunch of also-rans. Covenant distinctiveness is sustained (at least in part) by faithful marital practice. This was a concern long before torah-time. In Genesis 24 Abraham seems almost paranoid about Isaac getting a wife from Abraham's home turf rather than from the surrounding Canaanites (Gen. 24:3, 6). It's as if Abraham knew instinctively what would happen to the covenant seed if that seed contracted a deviant marriage.

This claim still rests upon Messiah's people – and can still prove costly. Gresham Machen was an eminent New Testament scholar in the fore part of the twentieth century, holding positions at Princeton and (later) Westminster seminaries. He was single throughout his life, but there was at one time a serious romantic relationship. The young woman was from Boston, one Machen described as 'intelligent, beautiful, exquisite.' But the relation never blossomed into engagement and marriage, because she was a Unitarian. Though Machen explained his Christian faith to her, gave her helpful reading material, she could never bring herself to share his faith. So the relationship ended.[5] Costly, sad – and yet faithful.

That steadfastness, however, can be the exception rather than the rule. At least it seems to have been that way in Ezra's present circumstances. He is really confessing and lamenting that Israel seems always to have had an allergy to distinctiveness – they do not want to be different but prefer to blend and mesh with the trappings of their culture. Hard to be 'holy.'

And yet there is something attractive about this covenant distinctiveness when it appears. In 1884 Grover Cleveland received the Democratic Party's nomination for President of the United States amid not unusual opposition. But the hall especially swung in Cleveland's favor when a former Wisconsin representative, Edward S. Bragg, made the 'seconding' speech. He referred to the young voters of Wisconsin and their pro-Cleveland attitude: 'They love him,

---

5. Ned B. Stonehouse, *J. Gresham Machen*, 3rd ed. (Edinburgh: Banner of Truth, 1987), 317-20.

gentlemen, and they respect him, not only for himself, for his character, for his integrity and judgment and iron will, but they love him most *for the enemies that he has made*.'[6] Ezra would have liked that. He was with a people who did not want to have an 'edge,' who did not want to *stand over against* their surrounding culture.

Secondly, we meet with **the embarrassing response of God's servant** (vv. 3-5). Maybe it was embarrassing to those who saw it, but I'm especially thinking of how contemporary western Christians might well look at it. Ever since 7:27 Ezra has been reporting in first-person form, and so he does here:

> 3. And when I heard this report, I ripped my clothes and my robe and pulled out some hair from my head and beard and sat down utterly stunned. 4. And to me were gathered everyone who trembled at the words of the God of Israel over the treachery of the exiles; and I went on sitting stunned until the evening sacrifice. 5. And at the time of the evening sacrifice I got up from my humiliation – with my clothes and robe torn – and fell on my knees and spread out my hands to Yahweh my God.

How might a modern reader, sitting at his kitchen table, sipping his morning coffee, be tempted to respond to this? Might he not say, 'Ezra, don't you think you are over-reacting, doing a bit of religious hyper-ventilating? Surely you're being too extreme; you're above and beyond here.' Well, we certainly think that no sane Presbyterian or Episcopalian would act that way.[7]

But Ezra is not alone. He is part of a fellowship of God-tremblers, others who, though not precisely imitating his actions, nevertheless share his disposition (v. 4). Their description comes from Isaiah 66:2 where Yahweh depicts his servants: 'But this is the one to whom I will look – to

---

6. Troy Senik, *A Man of Iron* (New York: Threshold Editions, 2022), 85-86 (emphasis mine).

7. Some scorned George Whitefield for so frequently weeping in his preaching. His response was: 'You blame me for weeping, but how can I help it when you will not weep for yourselves, though your immortal souls are on the verge of destruction, and for aught you know, you are hearing your last sermon, and may never more have an opportunity to have Christ offered to you' (Arnold A. Dallimore, *George Whitefield*, 2 vols. [Westchester, IL: Crossway, 1979], 2:483).

one afflicted and stricken in spirit, and who trembles at my word.' Still, Ezra is more than a bit embarrassing. We get terribly nervous when anyone is that frantic over sin. We could understand Ezra being a bit upset but being totally devastated and disabled over it – we can't quite fathom that. But then we find even 'extremism' over mercy unnerving.

I know I've noted it before, but I can't help but think of Bethan Lloyd-Jones' story about how her mother taught an illiterate elderly man named Mr Matthews to read. She taught him in Welsh. And it seemed like in no time that Mr Matthews was reading slowly, following his finger on the words. Soon he was quite at ease with it. Then when 'he first picked out the word Iesu [Jesus] he broke down completely, and with tears running down his cheeks, and crying, "Oh, his name, his blessed name!", he picked up the book and kissed that name.'[8] Had I been there, I would probably have been impressed – and uneasy, which would say more about me than Mr Matthews. A response like that is unsettling – gets too close to the dividing of joints and marrow. Just as Ezra's distress does to us. Unless we are among those who tremble at Yahweh's Word.

Thirdly, notice how even in the anguish of Ezra's prayer he highlights **the encouraging moment of God's grace** (vv. 8-9). He confesses he is almost too ashamed to pray. Our iniquities, he says, drown us, our guilt reaches all the way to heaven (v. 6) – and this has always been the case: 'From the days of our fathers we've been in massive guilt, to this day' (v. 7a). We've never been able to get it right. No wonder we've been 'given' to sword, captivity, and plundering (v. 7b). Then verse 8 begins with Ezra's 'And now …,' indicating a significant moment. The next phrase, lit., 'like a littleness of a moment,' shows that this 'moment' is a brief one – and it stands in contrast to the whole dominant history of unfaithfulness and judgment summarized in verse 7. What is so special about this 'brief moment'? Just that in it 'grace has been (shown) from Yahweh our God' (v. 8a). Let's take time to see how this grace is 'specked out.'

---

8. Lynette G. Clark, *Far Above Rubies* (Ross-shire: Christian Focus, 2015), 129.

It is the grace of *survival*; it is grace from Yahweh 'to leave us an escaped group.' The very fact that there *is* now a 'rump Israel' living here in Judah is testimony to that grace. It is the grace of *stability*: 'and to give us a peg in his holy place.' Most translations render the literal 'peg' metaphorically as something like 'secure place.' 'Peg' usually means a tent peg, driven into the ground as secure anchorage for a tent (cf. Isa. 54:2); or it could refer, as in Isaiah 22:23, to a peg or nail securely driven into a wall so that items could hang on it.[9] The 'peg' might refer to the rebuilt temple, as the following phrase ('in his holy place') might suggest.[10] The temple might be a sign of their 'anchorage,' but one that could be compromised and corrupted. In any case, the idea is that Israel has been given some degree of stability, of ballast, in her otherwise tenuous post-exilic existence.

Ezra's description rolls on with the grace of *encouragement*: 'that our God may give light to our eyes and give us a little reviving in our slavery' (v. 8b). Not big deliverance but 'a little reviving' – and that stirs hope. Then there is the grace of *constancy*, implied in verse 9a: 'For we are slaves, yet in our slavery our God has not forsaken us,' and this is followed by the grace of *providence* in verse 9b: 'he has extended his faithful love to us even under the kings of Persia and revived us to rebuild the Temple of our God, to restore its ruins' (NJB). All the drama and history of Ezra 1–6 is packed into that half-verse. And, finally, there is the grace of *protection:* 'to give us a wall in Judah and Jerusalem' (v. 9c). The 'wall' is metaphorical for protection; it is not likely a literal city wall since it is *'in Judah* and in Jerusalem.'

In Ezra's prayer, then, the immensity of guilt (vv. 6-7) is met by the massiveness of grace (vv. 8-9). 'But in our slavery our God has not forsaken us.' How Ezra can make us wallow in the un-let-go-able-ness of God. And yet Israel seems bent on scorning it away.

Now we come, finally, to **the perilous position before God's scrutiny** (vv. 13-15). 'The striking feature here is that

---

9. cf. A. Tomasino, NIDOTTE, 2:569-70.

10. D. J. A. Clines, *Ezra, Nehemiah, Esther*, NCBC (Grand Rapids: Eerdmans, 1984), 123.

the prayer is almost entirely confession with no real petition because Ezra is so conscious of sinfulness.'[11] There's no 'Amen.' A terribly untidy end of a prayer. Here Ezra brings us to the edge of a precipice. He suggests that if they go on with their commandment-breaking intermarriage, they may have reached the edge of God's patience (v. 14). If that should be the case, 'Will You not rage against us till we are destroyed without remnant or survivor?' (v. 14b, NJPS). Derek Kidner points out that this threat was no piece of maybe-stance: 'There were other Israelites scattered abroad, through whom the promises could be fulfilled.'[12] So Ezra confesses Yahweh is righteous (v. 15a) and we are guilty (v. 15b). End of prayer.

Ezra 9 in and of itself ends on this edge. This may bring up a question about whether in preaching or teaching we must always end on an 'up' note, with a 'gracious' note. I think I have heard that insisted on – that we must not leave people 'down' but give them a clear glimmer of hope and grace. But doesn't that take the cutting edge off the hard word the Spirit wants to impress? I don't think we must always feel compelled to provide folks with a parting psychological caress. Sometimes perhaps all we dare say is: 'Behold, we are before you in our guilt.'

Once more, it's all clear. If the church survives, it will be a wonder. After all, how can there be an escaped remnant between the enemies who hate us (chapters 1–6) and the sins we love (chapters 9–10)?

---

11. Robert Fyall, *The Message of Ezra and Haggai*, BST (Downers Grove, IL: Inter-Varsity, 2010), 124.

12. Derek Kidner, *Ezra and Nehemiah*, TOTC (Leicester: Inter-Varsity, 1979), 69.

9

A Hard Winter

(Ezra 10)

Let's say you've just had an accident in traffic. Two lanes going in the same direction. You pulled over into the other lane and swiped another vehicle you couldn't or didn't see in your 'blind spot.' So it's your fault. You and the other motorist are waiting for the police to arrive. It's 41 degrees (Fahrenheit; 5 Centigrade) – and raining. A bit of sheer misery. Something like December 19, 458 B.C. (cf. v. 9).[1] Folks in Judah were under strong pressure (vv. 7-8) to face up to a terrible wrong ('this matter,' v. 13) amid lousy weather, probably cold and certainly pouring rain (vv. 9, 13). Meteorology and guilt produced complex misery. What then can we observe in this occasion?

First, we meet with **a strange and sincere sorrow** (vv. 1, 6). The account continues from chapter 9 but switches by speaking of Ezra in the third person. Ezra still seems distraught and wild with grief – he keeps 'weeping and throwing himself down' (v. 1) in front of the temple. Ezra is beside himself in despair, and his intense anguish caught both the interest and concern of a huge number of folks (v. 1b). These people were not skeptical or critical of Ezra's demonstrative reaction. In fact, it was contagious – 'the people wept bitterly' as well.

However, we shouldn't miss the evident sincerity of Ezra here. He wasn't 'grand-standing' for the crowd. When he went into the temple complex, into the private chamber of

---

1. See Yamauchi, EBC, 4:454.

Jehohanan, away from the public view, he refused bread and water[2] and 'kept mourning over the treachery of the exiles' (v. 6). His anguish was not a bit of theatre; privacy is the litmus test of sincerity (cf. Zech. 12:12-14). What he was in public, he was in private.

Nor should Christ's contemporary disciples shy away from this matter of sorrow and mourning over sin. I find Ezekiel 36:31 so impressive and instructive in this matter. In that text Yahweh tells Israel what they will do when he restores them: 'And you shall remember your evil ways and your deeds that were not good, and you shall loathe yourselves over your iniquities and your abominations.' The Bible is so refreshingly unmodern. In an age that says such a response is unhealthy, Yahweh says, 'You shall loathe yourselves.' But this occurs (context!) precisely because Yahweh will put his Spirit within them (v. 27). So this new sadness (v. 31) is proof of the gift of a new Spirit. A very *proper* response then. Perhaps the apostle is an individual sample of this. Paul is so poignant in 1 Corinthians 15:9, when he says, 'I am not fit to be called an apostle, because I persecuted the church of God.' Was he forgiven? Yes. But, like Paul, the memory hangs on and rightly humbles us. Paul could never forget. And in the face of the therapeutic palaver of our age neither should we. There is a place for sincere sorrow before the house of God.

Secondly, in verses 2-4, we see – or hear – **a tenacious and heartening hope**. Was Ezra perhaps hoping for someone to respond as Shecaniah did? At any rate, Shecaniah speaks up; he refuses to despair[3] and proposes a way ahead through the morass (v. 3) with Ezra taking the lead (v. 4). Shecaniah's point is: Not all is lost; we can address this matter. What a boost he must have given Ezra's spirits!

But an observation: Shecaniah is a minor character. He's like so many others in the biblical story who appear for a moment of ministry and then disappear in their former obscurity – or who don't seem to be on the kingdom varsity

---

2. Like Moses when mourning and interceding 'forty days and forty nights' after Israel's 'calf' episode (Deut. 9:18).

3. The last phrase of his statement in verse 2 can be translated as 'in this matter' or as 'in spite of this.' Shecaniah's main contention, however, is that 'there is hope for Israel.'

squad. But how often 'minor characters' prove crucial, whether Nabal's unnamed servant (1 Sam. 25:14-17), or Mrs Naaman's cleaning girl (2 Kings 5:2-3), or Ebedmelech (Jer. 38-39), or Paul's nephew (Acts 23:16-22), or Epaphroditus (Phil. 2), or Onesiphorus (2 Tim. 1). And here it's Shecaniah with his 'But even now there is hope for Israel in spite of this,' putting fresh hope and energy into Ezra's soul.

God seems addicted to raising up and using 'minor' characters. Eugene Peterson tells how he was spiritually numb and unanchored after his second year of college. Even being back in his native Montana for the summer offered no 'cure.' Talking with his pastor and another 'saintly' man provided no help. A friend suggested Eugene might speak with Reuben Lance. But Lance was, well, formidable – overgrown eyebrows, wild red beard, burly and surly, and an all-around handyman. Peterson said you wanted him by your side in a dark alley, but you didn't go to him with an aching heart. Somehow Eugene got up the nerve to approach Reuben, told him how he was feeling, and asked if he could talk with him. Lance told him that if he wanted to do that to meet him in the church basement after supper on Tuesdays and Thursdays. Those unhurried conversations, the listening of that rough man, proved to be just the balm Peterson needed.[4] Reuben Lance, one of God's minor – and needed – characters. And now back to Ezra 10, where we should be saying, 'Praise be to God for the Shecaniahs who go around picking Yahweh's servants up off the floor!'

Third, we see here **a clear and severe demand** (vv. 7-11). The call goes out for an assembly at Jerusalem (v. 7) and, in case any should consider it low priority, a little pressure is added (v. 8). So, on December 19, the men of Judah and Benjamin stood in front of the temple, knowing what was coming, and soaked to the skin (v. 9). Ezra's words carry no nuanced padding. He moves from *accusation* ('You have committed treachery and married foreign wives,' 10), to *direction* ('And now give praise [or: make confession] to Yahweh, God of your fathers and do his will,' 11a), to *specification* ('and separate yourselves from the peoples of the lands – from the foreign wives,' 11b).

---

4. Winn Collier, *A Burning in My Bones* (n.p.: Waterbrook, 2021), 50-51.

The prophecy of Malachi *may* provide some background for the scene in Ezra 10. Malachi likely (in my view) prophesied a bit before Ezra's time and said that some of Judah's men had 'married the daughter of a foreign god' (Mal. 2:11), i.e., had married pagan women. Not only so, but, in order to be able to do so, they had wrongfully divorced their Jewish wives (Mal. 2:14). They trampled on their marriage covenant and married pagans. Perhaps they found a 'newer model,' or, more likely, enjoyed economic advantages from marrying into established and wealthier surrounding families. In any case, wrongful and heartless divorce had preceded a number of these foreign marriages.

Remember Ezra's demand is not driven by some panicked xenophobia but by a torah-mandated 'covenant phobia' (Exod. 34; Deut. 7). These marriages, of course, could involve all sorts of emotional and financial issues, but that is not the point here. Rather, Israel must decide (again) whether to be Yahweh's people or just another diluted near eastern religious club. Shucked to the core, does the first commandment matter? Apparently, not always. There was a Jewish colony at Elephantine in Egypt (contemporary with Ezra and Nehemiah); they engaged in intermarriage with locals and worshiped, for example, not only Yahweh but also the goddess Anath-Yahweh.[5] Ezra was right to be alarmed. Hence, 'Separate yourselves ... from the foreign wives' (v. 11). Severe but necessary.

Ezra's demand shows that emergency conditions require drastic measures. Once, in 1976, Governor Ronald Reagan was making a run for the US presidency. Once on the plane, after a campaign appearance, he asked the stewardess for a bag of peanuts and a Coke. He had a ritual – he'd pop a peanut in his mouth one at a time. Just as Reagan had popped another peanut, the plane took off; the force of the take-off pressed Reagan's head against the seat. His top aide, Mike Deaver, noted a pained, confused look on Reagan's face. The governor wrestled with and got his seat belt loosened, couldn't quite straighten up. His wife screamed, agents near him thought it was a heart attack, were grabbing for oxygen, while his

---

5. Yamauchi, EBC, 4:464.

face turned a dark red. Mike Deaver thought he knew what was happening, elbowed his way past the others, grabbed Reagan from behind and, with several hard wrenches under his rib cage, saw a peanut considerately pop out.[6] One doesn't usually manhandle a presidential candidate, but some occasions require drastic measures. So it was that winter day in Jerusalem.

Then, verses 12-17 show us that this whole affair was dealt with by **a wise and just procedure**. The offense required radical action, but that must not be carried out in a half-baked or madly precipitous manner. The assembly agreed with Ezra's proposal but raised two concerns: current conditions and required time. That is, the weather was wretched – no one wanted to risk pneumonia standing in a downpour – and the number of 'cases' would require an extended period of time to address. So, why not have an 'oversight committee,' set up a regimen of appointments for those who've been charged, and have elders and judges from the town of each man charged come and appear with him? See verse 14. Local officials would likely know of any ameliorating factors in an individual man's case. For example, what if a foreign wife had become a decided worshiper of Yahweh?[7] The investigative process took three months, which, given the number of cases and allowing for Sabbaths, works out to about one and a half cases per day.[8] A careful and orderly procedure.

This carefulness falls in with other potential or actual occasions in the Old Testament. According to Deuteronomy 13:12-18, if a city in Israel should apostatize, turn away from

---

6. Michael K. Deaver, *A Different Drummer* (New York: Perennial, 2003), 68-69. Ironically and providentially, about a month earlier Reagan himself had demonstrated this Heimlich maneuver to Deaver.

7. cf. F. C. Fensham, *The Books of Ezra and Nehemiah*, NICOT (Grand Rapids: Eerdmans, 1982), 140: 'Their local leaders and judges who knew their circumstances were to accompany them [the accused]. This last proposal is very important. The people wanted a fair investigation in which every case would be carefully scrutinized with the aid of leaders who had an intimate knowledge of the circumstances.'

8. Verse 15 indicates that there were several who were opposed to this procedure. We can't be sure about what they opposed. Some think they wanted more precipitous action and were against the extended process of interviews. Others think they were opposed to doing anything at all against those who had contracted foreign marriages. I lean toward the latter option.

worshiping Yahweh, the residents of said city were to be wiped out and the town nuked. But first Israel had to carefully investigate to see if the report of such apostasy was actually the case (v. 14). So too in Joshua 22. The 'west bank' Israelites heard that the eastern tribes had erected an altar near the Jordan, assumed it was an act of covenant infidelity, and prepared to go to war against the eastern tribes. But first they sent the Phinehas Commission to them to determine what exactly had occurred (Josh. 22:13ff.) and discovered there was no intent of apostasy.

In a general sense, then, Ezra 10 can still be a model for us in somewhat similar scenarios, for we can aim to do right but do it in such a way that leaves a good deal of damage. I remember hearing about my Uncle Bade (long 'a,' his name was Duane; don't know where 'Bade' came from) when Aunt Frank (she was really 'Frances,' but we called her Frank) was wanting to move her china cupboard. You've probably faced a similar situation: a piece of furniture looks like it will fit in a certain place but, when tried, doesn't quite do so. That was the way with Aunt Frank's china cupboard. But Uncle Bade was a resourceful fellow, laid hold of his sledgehammer, and gave the cupboard a good whack on the leg to force it into position. The force of the blow popped open the door and the china crackled out. Ezra insisted on a 'severe' solution but did not carry it out in a sledgehammer way.

Additional note: It seems to me that Ezra 10 does not provide a normative pattern for God's people today. We rightly get nervous over the idea of dissolving marriages and how this seems to fit ill with the overall biblical standard of the sanctity of marriage.[9] We must recognize, I suggest, that Ezra 9–10 represents a unique situation in redemptive history, when the 'church' faced an emergency situation, one involving the very survival of a faithful remnant, and so extreme measures

---

9. Some may object that Paul's advice in 1 Corinthians 7:12-13 counters Ezra 10, for he tells those in 'mixed' marriages not to divorce if the unbelieving spouse is willing to continue the marriage. But that is to mix up mixed marriages. The marriages Paul spoke of were originally those of two pagans. Then one of them is converted, believes in Jesus and the gospel, but the other partner remains pagan. The marriage becomes 'mixed' because of conversion to Christ. That's different from Ezra 9–10, where the marriages were mixed because a Jewish man (likely divorced his Jewish wife and) deliberately married a pagan.

were called for and taken. It was a 'one-off' affair. We are not required to imitate Ezra 10. There are, however, implications simply flowing from the general concern of Ezra 9–10. For example, if a pastor has a young man, a professing believer, in his congregation who wants him to perform the marriage for himself and his intended, and if the pastor, after meeting with them, determines the young lady neither makes nor has a Christian profession – does he not have to say he cannot marry them? And warn them against marriage under present conditions? It may not make him popular, but he has to have the guts to say that.

Finally, the Book of Ezra ends with a list! We have here **a haunting and sobering record** (vv. 18-44). No word about who the divorced women were or where they and any children (v. 3, cf. v. 44) went. But there is this listing of the offenders: priests in the lead (vv. 18-22), then Levites (v. 23), singers (v. 24a), gatekeepers (v. 24b), and laity (vv. 25-44).

It's as if the text is saying, here are those who were willing to seek their own advantage, to ignore the demands of the covenant, to compromise the integrity and purity of God's people. That may sound harsh. But there it is. And there are the names. There is Jarib, Jozabad, Telem, Izziah, Chelal – all of them printed starkly on the page. There's a bit of shame there that ought to haunt us for our good.

We find the same sort of thing in the New Testament, though not in extended lists. One wonders if Euodia and Syntyche would blush if they knew readers of Philippians 4 would always remember them for their little spat. Or there's Demas, who, 'having loved the present age,' left Paul in the lurch (2 Tim. 4:10). No need to speculate about his final state. A. W. Tozer said all that needs to be said: the last time we see Demas he is facing the wrong way. But there is his name. And there is that royal pain in the church, Diotrephes (3 John 9-10), who loved the limelight and to throw his weight around. Such names, these or those in Ezra 10, should serve as amber-colored caution-lights to us, driving us to pray that the Lord would keep our names from ever besmirching his honor.

NEHEMIAH

10

Re-setting the Setting
(Nehemiah 1:1-3)

Let's allow the first verses of Nehemiah to re-orient us to the Ezra–Nehemiah account, as Nehemiah introduces himself and his times in 1:1-3. We are snooping in someone else's diary – 'the words of Nehemiah, son of Hacaliah' (v. 1).[1] A good bit of Nehemiah is a first-person account, an 'I' account. Not all but most of chapters 1–7, part of chapter 12 and most of 13. If an overall 'editor' was responsible for shaping Ezra–Nehemiah, we might imagine him saying to himself, 'Hmm, here are these "Nehemiah memoirs," and who can tell the story with more interest and drama than the primary human actor himself?' So he takes over Nehemiah's own account for the bulk of the story. After all, the man was in the thick of it.

Note that from these verses we are reminded that **Nehemiah provides us with a selective account.** If the twentieth year of verse 1b is the twentieth year of Artaxerxes I, then we are in *c.* 445 B.C. Comparing Ezra 7:7, we note that this was thirteen years after Ezra's coming (458 B.C.). So, clearly, the whole complex of Ezra–Nehemiah is not meant as a complete report of affairs in post-exilic Judah; the treatment is *episodic,* often with the passage of years between key moments in the narrative. Those 'key moments' are the focal points in the

---

1. Some prefer 'deeds' (Goswell) or 'narrative' (REB, NJPS) to 'words,' but I've stuck to the last.

main 'chunks' (Ezra 1–6; 7–10; Neh. 1–7; 8–13) of the overall account, each 'chunk' highlighting some major difficulty, crisis, or discouragement faced by the Lord's remnant. A sort of preview of Acts 14:22b. Since the report is selective, it means we don't have all the data we'd like to have for solving historical conundrums and/or for answering our puzzling questions. This fact should be a caution light to us, and especially to negative critics, about pontificating about some item being 'unhistorical' or a certain passage being out of place. We need to be restrained in our judgment since we don't have exhaustive coverage. One might say there are missing links in the evolution of the account.

Nehemiah provides us with very basic background information. The current moment was the month Chislev, November–December. He was in Susa in what is now SW Iran, in the alluvial plain 150 miles north of the Persian Gulf. Susa served as the winter palace for the Persian kings. But there is further background that is helpful in that it shows that **Nehemiah's labors occur in the wake of chaotic times**, simply something we should appreciate. Perhaps it's best just to itemize some of these matters:

1. Artaxerxes' father, Xerxes, was assassinated in his bedchamber in 465 B.C., by Artabanus, a powerful courtier.

2. There was a revolt by his brother Hystaspes in Bactria (far to the NE) at the beginning of Artaxerxes' reign.

3. In 460 B.C. there was a revolt in Egypt, supported by the Athenians, which took five years to put down. For this reason Artaxerxes I may have been only too glad to send Ezra to Palestine to ensure a loyal buffer state in Judah.

4. In 448 B.C., Megabyzus, satrap of Trans-Euphrates (and brother-in-law of Artaxerxes), rebelled. Megabyzus had put down the revolt in Egypt led by one Inarus; Megabyzus promised to spare Inarus' life but the latter was impaled at the instigation of Artaxerxes' mother. This ticked off Megabyzus; hence his revolt (though he was later reconciled to Artaxerxes).

If the events of Ezra 4:7-23 took place during this time in Artaxerxes' reign, one can understand his paranoia about allowing Jerusalem to be fortified.

5. By 445 B.C. these revolts had ended. Perhaps that explains why there was no objection to Nehemiah's rebuilding Jerusalem's walls at such a time.[2]

Such matters of historical context can prove useful, if nothing more than to alert us that things are usually more complicated than they seem. Stable and sedate did not always describe the Persian empire.

Finally, note that **Nehemiah's task is stimulated by depressing news** (vv. 2-3). And note how Nehemiah pitches his inquiry of Hanani and his colleagues – he asks about the condition of the people before he asks about the city itself (v. 2).[3] Perhaps that's incidental but it may be revealing. In any case, he receives a distressing answer:

> The survivors who have survived the captivity there in the province are in dire trouble and disgrace; Jerusalem's wall is full of breaches, and its gates have been destroyed by fire (v. 3, NJPS).

The usual view is that all this refers to what happened in Ezra 4:23, since a somewhat more recent event was more likely to be news to Nehemiah. But there's still much reason to hold that these conditions reflect the abiding devastation inflicted by the Babylonians in 587 B.C.[4]

Such depressing news depresses Nehemiah (see v. 4). Somehow life cannot continue in its usual equilibrium when he realizes the severe duress the remnant in Judah is enduring. And yet, if considered in a strictly objective way, his concern might be a bit surprising.

---

2. For some of these items, see Edwin M. Yamauchi, *Persia and the Bible* (Grand Rapids: Baker, 1990), 248-51.

3. W. J. Martin, ZPEB, 4:404.

4. Note C. F. Keil, *The Books of Ezra, Nehemiah, and Esther*, Biblical Commentary on the Old Testament (reprint ed., Grand Rapids: Eerdmans, 1966), 156-59; also F. C. Fensham, *The Books of Ezra and Nehemiah*, NICOT (Grand Rapids: Eerdmans, 1982), 152.

Dr Donald Grey Barnhouse told of a time in the 1940s when he was driving to Pensacola, Florida. He'd preached twelve times that week, just driven 300 miles, and now had a flat tire. He was exhausted, but a fellow came along in a jeep and Barnhouse offered to pay him to change the flat. The young man had a yellow mongrel dog with him; he nuzzled the fellow as he worked, would get pushed back, and then return to nuzzle him once more. Barnhouse remarked (in what would become a gospel opportunity) that man and dog seemed on excellent terms. His mechanic du jour told how the dog had once appeared out of nowhere when he was stuck in quicksand and had been the means of freeing him. So the dog could have anything he wanted! He ate with him and, to his wife's chagrin, he slept with them. Barnhouse asked what he might do if some guy down at the nearby store would kick his dog. 'Mister, I believe I'd kill him.'[5] Well, one can understand his gratitude and affection. And yet someone else unaware of the whole story could be unimpressed with the animal. What was he? A yellow cur, a nondescript canine mutt. Why would he solicit any solicitude?

In one sense, isn't there a bit of a marvel in Nehemiah's angst over the folks in Jerusalem? Why should he care for a bunch of 'survivors'? Why should he burden himself over some no-count folks in an out-of-the-way corner of the Persian empire? He has himself a cushy government post in Susa, and there's no reason, is there, for him to make himself miserable over a bunch of miserable Jews? It's a bit surprising. And yet perfectly proper. For God's true servants always prize God's people, especially the 'least' of them. It's an instinct that reflects the disposition of a God who delights to choose no-counts and rejects (1 Cor. 1:26-29; James 2:5).

---

5. Donald Grey Barnhouse, *Let Me Illustrate* (Westwood, NJ: Fleming H. Revell, 1967), 149-51.

11

Knowing Prayer
(Nehemiah 1:4-11)

Once, when one of our sons came home for a visit he made a statement about some matter in the current news that surprised his mother. Naturally she asked how he could claim what he asserted. In a bit of a spoof, he narrowed his eyes and insisted, with an aura of mystery, 'I know things.' The same could be said of Nehemiah in his prayer (vv. 5-11). Verse 4 indicates that Nehemiah's distress over Judah and Jerusalem went on for some time: 'I sat down and I was weeping and mourning for days, and I was fasting and praying before the God of heaven.' The prayer of verses 5-11, then, is a *sample* of what his prayers were like during this time. But it's clear from this sample prayer that Nehemiah 'knows things.' We could say he engages in knowing prayer.

He knows, for example, **the God to whom he prays** (vv. 5-6a). He addresses Yahweh as 'God of heaven, the great and fearful God' – he is the 'awe-full' God. Yet since he is 'keeping covenant and faithful love toward those who love him and keep his commands,' he is also the 'faith-full' God, committing himself to his people. Put these two 'attributes' together and note how they complement one another: great and fearful, keeping covenant and faithful love. God is both scary and dependable. But then Nehemiah assumes he is also the 'approachable' God, for he can be spoken to! 'Let now your ear pay attention and your eyes be open to hear the prayer of your servant ....' As one of my friends used to say, 'You can talk to Yahweh!' Here is the welcome miracle of an accessible God.

Charles Hodge was the stalwart theologian of Princeton Seminary in the nineteenth century. His study was in his house, with one entrance toward the seminary and the other to the inner parts of the house. His son's account of his life says that at every age and at all times his children were 'allowed free access to him.' Time came when he even took the latch from the doors and they would swing open via springs, so that even a toddler could waddle in, unhindered, to his father.[1] Don't we assume something like that is the case every time we pray? That the 'awe-full' and 'faith-full' God is at the same time approachable?

Note then *where prayer begins:* with the knowledge of the nature of the covenant God. The character of God is the bedrock for prayer. *Theology* is the proper foundation for *devotion.*

Secondly, Nehemiah shows that **he knows the sin in which he shares**. A major part of his prayer consisted in 'confessing the sins of the sons of Israel, which we have sinned against you, both I and my father's house have sinned; we have acted very corruptly against you and we have not kept the commandments and statutes and rules which you commanded Moses your servant' (vv. 6b-7). Note the repeated first-person plural 'we' throughout. Nehemiah is claiming no exemption from the guilt of Israel, as if all of it belonged to previous deviant generations. No, we have sinned ... I and my father's house ... we have acted very corruptly. They know this because their offenses have been committed in violation of revelation received through Moses, like Christian in Bunyan's *Pilgrim's Progress*, who knew about the burden on his back 'by reading this book.' So, Nehemiah does not duck his part in original, historical, corporate, and personal sin. He's not like the clueless tutor who says, 'Don't use no double negatives, and, last but not least, lay off cliches.'[2]

---

1. A. A. Hodge, *The Life of Charles Hodge* (1880; reprint ed., Edinburgh: Banner of Truth, 2010), 104, 244.

2. Thanks to Dr Roy Taylor, former colleague at Reformed Seminary, for this clip from his preaching syllabus.

One fears that the contemporary church has largely lost such grieving over sin. You can see it in its 'worship' services. These frequently consist of thirty minutes of singing with the amplifier turned up, a brief prayer, then an exposition by a communicator topped off with several 'take away' points, followed by a closing prayer. But there is no 'Prayer of Confession' in the service; they've no idea what that is. Granted, a prayer of confession can be rote, trite, and merely formal, but the fact that it is almost wholly foreign to many churches is revealing. Of course, church folks would agree with the culture at large that 'nobody's perfect,' but one wonders if we are as naïve and ignorant as the man who came to Jesus and was utterly blind to his hidden idolatry (Mark 10:20ff.). Perhaps Jesus is still saying to his church: 'You do not know that you are wretched and pitiable and poor and blind and naked' (Rev. 3:17).

The third observation about Nehemiah's prayer is that **he knows the promise on which he pleads** (vv. 8-9). Back in verse 7 Nehemiah had referred to the commandments, statutes, and rules Yahweh had 'commanded Moses your servant.' Now in verse 8 he mentions a *dabar,* a promise, that Yahweh 'commanded Moses your servant.' In verses 8b-9 Nehemiah quotes the gist of that promise: 'should **you** commit treachery, **I** will scatter you among the peoples, and when you shall turn to me and keep my commandments and shall do them – if your banished ones are at the end of the heavens, from there I will gather them and bring them to the place I have chosen to make my name dwell.'[3] Nehemiah seems to be drawing upon Deuteronomy 30, particularly verses 3-5. That chapter displays Yahweh's ultimate Covenant Recovery Program. The first of the chapter moves from foreign banishment (v. 1), to full-bore repentance (v. 2) and on to invincible restoration (vv. 3-5). Deuteronomy 30:4 especially seems to feed into Nehemiah's prayer: 'Even if your banished ones are at the end of the heavens, from there Yahweh your God will gather you and from there he will take you.'

---

3. I have translated the opening of verse 9 as 'when' (with Steinmann), rather than 'if' as most English versions.

Deuteronomy 30 seems to say that this restoration will in fact come about. Verse 2 in that text rests on the assumption that the people will in fact return to Yahweh.[4] Verse 8 carries the same definite tone: 'but you, you will return and shall listen to the voice of Yahweh ....' So when Nehemiah alludes to the Deuteronomy 30 context and pleads for Yahweh to 'remember now the promise you commanded Moses your servant' (Neh. 1:8), he seems to be asking that that promise be fulfilled (or at least begin to be fulfilled) in his own time.

What is important to see here is that *prayer is based on promises.* Prayer takes hold of God's promises, turns them into petitions, and sends them back to God. Nehemiah has every reason then to expect God's favorable reply.

Fourthly, Nehemiah **knows the history to which he can appeal** (v. 10). Israel's God is no Johnny-come-lately. Yahweh has made and shaped history. And he has a history with Nehemiah's people: 'and they are your servants and your people whom you redeemed with your great power and strong hand' (cf. the language of Moses' intercession in Deuteronomy 9:29). Nehemiah not only claims a promise (vv. 8-9) but recalls a history (v. 10), which he uses as an argument. It's as if he says, 'Look, Lord, at the investment you have poured into this people; will you allow the brute power with which you freed them from the clutches of Egypt to fizzle out during the tenure of Persia?' Solomon made a like appeal in 1 Kings 8:51 in its context.

Analogies pale almost to triviality, but help us grasp the principle involved. Shelby Foote has authored a narrative history of the American Civil War. He says he began writing it in 1954, finished in 1974, and did little else during those twenty years. He says he used a 'dip pen' when writing his draft. That's the sort one used to find in US post offices – or that, long ago, elementary school students used for practicing 'penmanship.' One dipped the point in ink, wrote several words, till one had to dip again. Foote said that writing that way slowed him down,

---

4. 'The sentence is not conditional, but simply a continuation of the temporal clauses with which the chapter begins (i.e., not if, but when)' (Chris Wright, *Deuteronomy*, New International Biblical Commentary [Peabody, MA: Hendrickson, 1996], 289).

which, apparently, he needed.[5] Twenty years of dip-pen writing, not to mention research, producing three volumes totaling nearly 3,000 pages. At the end of that, could we imagine him saying, 'Well, I don't know; maybe I won't publish this; maybe I'll just let it rest on my library shelf.' No, there's something about heavy investment that drives one on. And that is the essence of Nehemiah's appeal to the spectacular redemption Yahweh accomplished in Egypt. Will he then back off and simply allow his people to piddle around as best they can? Not hardly. And, of course, in the present age he has invested in his people with a far greater redemption. He has executed a Golgotha-cross and garden-tomb redemption. Will he likely let that go for nothing? Will he allow his people to waddle along as best they can while they become extinct under the tyrants and terrorists of this age? Not hardly.

Now a last observation about Nehemiah: **he knows the crisis in which he stands** (v. 11). Nehemiah comes back to the 'hearing' concern of verse 6. Behind him, driving him on, is the grave condition of the people of Judah (v. 3); in front of him is the suspense over what the king's reaction might be. I'll split up our discussion under several considerations.

First, *time*. Nehemiah is preparing to broach his request to the king, and, according to 2:1, he does this in the month Nisan of Artaxerxes' twentieth year. Details get a bit sticky here.[6] However, it seems clear that there was a spread of about four months from the time Nehemiah heard the news about Judah

---

5. Brian Lamb, *Booknotes* (New York: Times Books, 1997), 8-10.

6. If we assume that the 'twentieth year' of 1:1 is the twentieth year of Artaxerxes I's reign (the text does not specifically say so), then there seems to be a rub with 2:1. The month Chislev (1:1) would be the ninth month on Israel's calendar and Nisan (2:1) would be the first month of the *next* year. Either the twentieth year of 2:1 should be the twenty-first, or, as some hold, the twentieth year of 1:1 should be actually the nineteenth. Several explanations have been offered. Perhaps the most feasible is that in Williamson, who draws on Bickerman's work, that Nehemiah, being in court circles, was following a regnal rather than a calendar year. Bickerman held that Artaxerxes came to the throne in the month of Ab (July-August), so if one thinks in terms of, say, an August-to-August year, then Chislev would be the fifth month and the following Nisan the ninth month, both fitting into that regnal twentieth year. See H. G. M. Williamson, *Ezra, Nehemiah*, WBC (Waco: Word, 1985), 170. cf. also William H. Shea, 'A Review of the Biblical Evidence for the Use of the Fall-to-Fall Calendar,' *Journal of the Adventist Theological Society* 12/2 (Autumn 2001): 161-62.

in the month Chislev (1:1) to the moment in the month Nisan (2:1) when he expressed his sorrow and petition to Artaxerxes. This shows that his action was not precipitous, not some sudden knee-jerk affair. Rather, this concern had been a matter of extended prayer. He prayed about this for four months.

Next, *community*. Nehemiah asks for Yahweh's attention not merely to *his* petitions but 'to the prayer of your servants who delight to fear your name.' Nehemiah did not stand alone in this venture; he had a cadre of intercessors who joined him in assaulting the throne of grace. One can imagine several fellows ambling along to Nehemiah's palace apartment on Tuesday and Thursday evenings for 'Jerusalem prayer meetings.'

Third, think of the matter of *perspective*. Nehemiah goes on to pray, 'And please give your servant success today, and give him compassions before this man.' Nehemiah is on the edge of broaching his burden to the king, the king who had previously put the 'shut' on the rebuilding of Jerusalem (Ezra 4:17-23). And Nehemiah is about to ask him to reverse that policy. Here is the autocratic Persian king – and Nehemiah calls him 'this man.'[7] A very accurate perspective, but one we sometimes find hard to hold.

Indeed, the arrogance of kings themselves tends to keep them from seeing themselves that way. The weak Louis XVI once silenced a dissenter with 'It is legal because it is my will.'[8] And James I (VI of Scotland) made no bones of semi-divinity when he once addressed Parliament:

> Kings are justly called gods, for that they exercise a manner or resemblance of divine power on earth; for if you will consider the attributes of God, you shall see how they agree in the person of a king. God hath power to create or destroy, make or unmake at His pleasure, to give life or send death, to judge all and be judged nor accountable to none ... And the like power have kings; they make and unmake their subjects, have power of raising and casting down, of life and death ....[9]

---

7. Compare the way David demotes the massive Goliath, dubbing him 'this Philistine' (1 Sam. 17:26).

8. Jay Winik, *The Great Upheaval* (New York: HarperCollins, 2007), 108.

9. Quoted in Will and Ariel Durant, *The Age of Reason Begins*, The Story of Civilization, Part VII (New York: Simon and Schuster, 1961), 138.

Andrew Melville's pulling on the royal sleeve and calling him 'God's silly vassal' never sunk in.

Where does Nehemiah's 'this man' leave us? It means we respect proper authority but we do not cringe before it. Artaxerxes I is the king. But he is also 'this man.' There is something very liberating in that point of view. It's the same attitude that oozes out of those words to Pontius Pilate: 'You would have no authority over me at all unless it had been given you from above' (John 19:11, ESV).

Fourth, in telling of this crucial moment Nehemiah touches on the matter of *providence:* 'and I was a king's cupbearer.' This is new information for us. This remark explains how it is that Nehemiah will have access to the king. The text doesn't tell us how Nehemiah obtained this position. But there he is.

This position was one of great responsibility and influence. Kings longed for reliable court attendants because of frequent intrigues at court. Artaxerxes' own father, Xerxes, had been assassinated in his own bedchamber by a court attendant. Wariness and security concerns prevailed – hence having dependable 'inner circle' personnel was crucial. As for 'cup-bearing' itself, Xenophon reports that when cupbearers would offer the wine to the king, they would first draw some of it off with a ladle, pour it into their left hand, and swallow it down, so that, if the cupbearer (or someone else?) had put poison in it, he would get his everlasting. Moreover, the cupbearer's closeness to the king probably meant he had some influence over who got access to the king.[10]

When Nehemiah makes his cupbearer remark, is he not recognizing that Yahweh's providence has been at work long before this tense moment? He was high up in the civil service with access to the king, and, therefore, was in a favorable position to seek good for the people of Judah. Who could doubt that he may have come to the kingdom for such a time as this (Esther 4:14b)?

Keep in view the first picture of Nehemiah that these memoirs give us: not the man who builds or organizes or governs – but the man who prays.

---

10. For all of this, see Edwin M. Yamauchi, *Persia and the Bible* (Grand Rapids: Baker, 1990), 259-60.

12

From Court to City
(Nehemiah 2)

Once there was a potato chip (Brits = crisps) advertisement that claimed, 'Bet you can't eat just one.' And if one likes potato chips, that's true. One can't be content with just one; there's a sort of primeval urge for more. Sometimes biblical accounts are like that. As we read, we think we simply must have 'more.' Especially in moments of intense suspense. Like the end of Nehemiah 1. Nehemiah informs us that he is a cupbearer to the king and with his 'today' that something very critical is about to happen. We can't be content with that; we can't stop reading; we must have 'more'; in our literary impatience we plunge on into chapter 2 to see what develops. Not that this is Nehemiah's 'fault.' It's not like he said, 'I think I'll end chapter 1 on this tense note and then start a new chapter.' Our (usually) helpful chapter and verse divisions are relatively recent (thirteenth–sixteenth centuries), but when they are marked out as they are, they sometimes leave us hanging at the end of a chapter – and so guarantee that we'll keep reading![1] And so we are in chapter 2 to see how it all turns out.

Before going into detail, observe the overall bifid structure of the chapter:

Vv. 1-10   Before the king, 1-4
           Favorable decision by king, 5-8
           Reaction of enemies, 9-10

---

1. Note how Exodus 1 leaves us dangling at the end of a rope (v. 22).

Vv. 11-20   Around the walls, 11-16
            Favorable decision by people, 17-18
            Reaction of enemies, 19-20

And note that in the second segment of both sections there is reference to the 'hand of my God' (vv. 8, 18). The account is carefully put together.

There also seems to be a play on terms throughout the chapter, more apparent in the Hebrew text. There are seven uses of terms relating to *ra'a'*, either adjective, noun, or as a verb. The root can carry a wide range of meanings. Usually in verses 1, 2, and 3 it is translated 'sad' or 'sadness.' However, we are more accustomed to thinking of what is 'evil' or 'bad' with this word group – as in verse 10, literally, 'It was evil to them [Nehemiah's enemies] a great evil.' Or it can connote 'distress' or 'misery,' as in verse 17 ('You see the distress we are in'). On the other hand, there are eight occurrences of the *tob* root, good, be good, pleasing (twice in v. 5, vv. 6, 7, 8; v. 10 = 'good' in the sense of 'welfare'; twice in v. 18, the second time = good work). All this may not be of overwhelming significance but the subtle undertow of evil/good should not be missed.

Our main concern, however, is with the 'testimony' of Nehemiah 2, which can be summarized under four main heads. And so, first, we need to trace **the good hand of God's providence** in verses 1-8. We can walk through these verses in several steps.

First off, we meet *sadness and fear* in verses 1-3. Some may wonder why it took Nehemiah almost four months (1:1 with 2:1) to make his concern known to the king. But there is just so much we don't know – we don't have the 'filler' for all the gaps we think we see. Artaxerxes could have been absent from Susa for part of the time; or Nehemiah's assignment for service in the cupbearer 'rotation' may not have been immediate. On this 'today' (1:11), however, Nehemiah's heaviness of spirit was apparent. He tells us that this had not happened before (v. 1b). Well, it wasn't supposed to be; court etiquette required that those near the royal presence display a convivial or cheerful demeanor.[2] Did Nehemiah

---

2. cf. the 'rule' laid upon guests in William Randolph Hearst's household: 'Never mention death in Mr Hearst's presence' (Marvin Olasky, *Prodigal Press* [Westchester, IL: Crossway, 1988], 54).

deliberately let his depression show in order to arouse the king's attention? Or had the matter so weighed him down over the weeks that he could not completely conceal his heaviness of heart? Nehemiah wasn't sick. It was obviously 'sadness of heart' (v. 2).

Some think the king may have been suspicious of Nehemiah (was he disgruntled?), but I think not. Most commentators don't say much about the king's comment. But it seems to me that it points to a slice of the king's humanity. Nehemiah, he recognizes, is depressed. Is it too much to assume that, given Nehemiah's faithful service, Artaxerxes may have come to have a kindly attachment toward him? Can't a wine-slurping, harem-loving, me-centered monarch sometimes show a sliver of care for someone? I recall when I was about twelve years old, my 'number three' brother (twelve years older) was home from the army. He was an avid fan of the St. Louis Cardinals baseball club and especially high on their all-star, Stan Musial. My favorite ball player was Alvin Dark, who at the time also played shortstop for the Cardinals. Dark was a fine ball player but not in the class of a Musial. Whenever I would praise the virtues of Dark, my brother would rifle me with statistics to show that Dark could not touch the hem of Musial's garment. He was right, but he was also severe in pounding home his evidence. One day my brother had come home from Pittsburgh – the Cardinals had been in town playing the Pittsburgh Pirates and my brother had been to the game. He came out of the house to go somewhere, saw me, and said, 'Well, Ralph, your man Alvin Dark had three hits today.' Tears came to my eyes; he had said it kindly; I wasn't used to that. And we're not used to monarchs taking a nub of personal interest in anyone who serves them, but it seems Artaxerxes did so, at least that day.

Nehemiah then is very afraid (v. 2b), perhaps due to his breach of court mores and perhaps even more because of the matter he was going to raise: 'Why should my face not be sad when the city, the place of the graves of my fathers, lies in ruins with its gates eaten up with fire?' (v. 3). There, it's out.[3]

---

3. Many expositors think Nehemiah quite suave here in that he did not mention Jerusalem by name. But I'm not sure that is such a big deal. The king may well have known Nehemiah's 'roots.'

In the next segment we find *tension and prayer* (vv. 4-6a). One nail-biter passes and here comes another! For when the king says, 'What are you seeking?', the answer is: 'the total reversal of your previous policy to stifle the rebuilding of Jerusalem' (see Ezra 4:21-22). That takes a bit of gall – which is why Nehemiah didn't speak to Artaxerxes first. Rather he says, 'Then I prayed to the God of heaven' (v. 4b). Some call it ejaculatory prayer or an 'arrow' prayer. It's that in-the-moment silent plea, 'Help, Lord!' But this sort of prayer has a context. Nehemiah *had been praying* about these matters for months (see 1:4ff.). On-the-spot prayer is based on ongoing prayer.[4] And here it shows the instinctive dependence Nehemiah has on God's help. Here is the balance between dependence and boldness: 'I prayed to the God of heaven,' dependence; 'and I said to the king ...,' boldness. He makes his request (v. 5) and receives the royal permission (v. 6a).[5]

All of this brings us to *preparation and providence* (vv. 6b-8). Who knows, humanly speaking, what moved Artaxerxes to reverse his previous policy about Jerusalem? Possibly having a loyal lieutenant ensuring stability to a chunk of turf on the western edges of the empire struck the king as an advantage.[6] At any rate, Nehemiah immediately requests official letters/credentials (v. 7) and authorization to obtain necessary construction materials (v. 8a). Obviously, Nehemiah's time had not all been taken up with lamentation and prayer – he had also already planned and calculated all that he would require for the task, should permission be granted. And granted it was – even for these additional requests, and the credit for it

---

4. Derek Thomas puts it well: 'Instant prayer of this nature arose only because Nehemiah had taught himself the value of prayer by a consistent *life* of prayer. Such reflex responses as this do not just occur; they are the result of a life lived in God's presence day by day. Nehemiah prayed this way because he was always praying this way' (*Ezra & Nehemiah* REC [Phillipsburg, NJ: P & R, 2016], 222).

5. Some make a good deal of the queen's presence (v. 6a) on this occasion. It may have been the queen or perhaps a favorite consort. Women seem to have had some influence in the machinations of the Persian court, and some think perhaps the queen or consort had pro-Nehemiah sentiments. There is no way of knowing. The allusion to the queen might simply be – no disparagement intended – due to the fact that she was there!

6. Or cf. also Edwin M. Yamauchi, *Persia and the Bible* (Grand Rapids: Baker, 1990), 250-51.

belongs, as Nehemiah confesses, to 'the good hand of my God upon me' (v. 8b).

That note of God's providence not only explains the king's assent to Nehemiah's additional request but also explains the whole reversal of Artaxerxes' previous policy (remember Ezra 4:21-22). 'The king's heart is channels of water in the hand of Yahweh – he turns it wherever he pleases' (Prov. 21:1). If Nehemiah had been apprehensive, he had every right to be so. What likelihood was there that the king would be willing to reverse his own explicit policy? But there is 'the hand of Yahweh.' It brings to mind Augustus Toplady's reflection on his own conversion:

> Strange that I, who had so long sat under the means of grace in England, should be brought nigh to God in an obscure part of Ireland, amidst a handful of God's people met together in a barn, and under the ministry of one who could hardly spell his name! Surely it was the Lord's doing, and is marvellous![7]

That is the case here. Not likely, but … 'it was the Lord's doing, and is marvellous.' It was the good hand of God's providence.

Secondly, this report shows **the keen wisdom of God's servant** (vv. 9-10, 11-16). Notice how – all of a sudden – Nehemiah is there! There is no narrative 'down time' between Persia and arriving in 'Beyond the River.' As so often in biblical narrative, there are no details of the journey. Biblical narrative has such an 'impatience' to get on with the story.

Right away one sees Nehemiah's wisdom in the manner of his arrival (v. 9). At various stops he presents his credentials; then he notes that 'the king also sent army officers and cavalry with me' (v. 9b, NJPS). Derek Kidner astutely says:

> There was more than protection to be gained from the military escort. It meant an arrival in style, impressively reinforcing the presentation of credentials to the neighbouring governors, and making very plain the change of royal policy.[8]

---

7. Nick Needham, *2000 Years of Christ's Power*, 5 vols. (Ross-shire: Christian Focus, 2023), 5:150.

8. Derek Kidner, *Ezra and Nehemiah*, TOTC (Leicester: Inter-Varsity, 1979), 81.

This display would not eliminate hostility (v. 10) but would likely temper its manifestations. It so much as said to Sanballat *et al.*, 'I've got government backing for this, so you'd better cool your heels.' Once we see this, we won't try to compare Nehemiah unfavorably with Ezra. Ezra and his band refused to ask for a military escort on their journey (Ezra 8:21-23) since they had claimed before the king that their God was sufficient to keep them secure. But Nehemiah's circumstances are different. Ezra needed to demonstrate the protection of God around them, while Nehemiah needed to show the support of the empire behind him. Ezra rejected an escort as a matter of faith, Nehemiah required one as a matter of wisdom. All of which should prove instructive for God's people in any age and keep us from hastily disparaging believers who follow a different track than we have. Sometimes one direction is faithful, while another time another direction is wise, without being unfaithful. At such times we are not practicing 'situation ethics' but circumstantial wisdom.

Nehemiah's wisdom also appears in his exercise of secrecy (vv. 11-16). He is going to survey the condition of and damage in Jerusalem. It is a Jerusalem probably restricted to the Hill Ophel (the southeastern hill) with the temple mount on the north of it. It seems he goes out the Valley Gate on the west side, goes south toward the Serpent's Well and the Dung Gate (v. 13a), circles round by the Fountain Gate (v. 14) and up the east side of the hill, where the mass of the collapsed eastern slope forced him to go on foot (v. 14b). Then he apparently re-traced his route and came back to the Valley Gate (v. 15b).[9]

All this in a blanket of secrecy. (You might even want to read verses 12-16 in a whisper.) Three times Nehemiah stresses his survey was at night (vv. 12, 13, 15), with only one animal – the one he rode (v. 12b), and only 'a few men' with him (v. 12a). Twice he insists that he 'did not tell'/'had not told' (vv. 12, 16) anyone, and that the 'officials did not know' where he had gone or what he had done (v. 16a).

---

9. One might think he would have kept going north and made a complete circuit, but it may well be that he could observe by day the condition of the wall near the temple; knowing the damage on the southern end was likely his main concern. For a helpful sketch/map, see *The Macmillan Bible Atlas*, 3rd. ed. (New York: Macmillan, 1993), 129.

All this was necessary. Nehemiah had never lived in Jerusalem and needed to get first-hand, close-up knowledge of its condition. He needed exact data first; then, if folks had objections, he could cogently answer. He needed to make this assessment on his own without other folks inserting their opinions into the matter. Committees are usually dangerous. Moreover, some of the Jews had contacts with surrounding peoples and, had they known of Nehemiah's plan, 'leaks' would have occurred.[10] At this point Nehemiah knew that secrecy was essential for success.

During the American War between the states, Confederate General Stonewall Jackson was in a pickle. It was March 1862. Jackson wanted to hold Winchester, Virginia, but Federal troops were closing in and Jackson was outnumbered six to one. His troops were marching south and away from the town. Then Jackson held a pow-wow with his senior commanders. He told them he planned to turn about and attack the Yankees the next day. They would be caught by surprise, disorganized, and over-confident and could be routed. His commanders demurred. The troops would have to march all night, six miles back to town in order to attack at daybreak. Jackson was sure it could be done but his associates persuaded him otherwise – and Jackson joined the retreat. But before Jackson left the environs of Winchester, he told a close friend, 'That is the last council of war I will ever hold.'[11] And it was – sometimes to the consternation and frustration of his underlings. But one can understand Stonewall. Let brigadiers discuss plans and they will see all the potential dangers and possible disasters to occur if this is done or that is tried. They are so mired in caution. So from that time on Jackson vowed secrecy, so that *audacity* would have a chance. It was a sort of 'Nehemiah technique.'

Wisdom does not usually collect plaudits; power is what gets the applause. But wisdom is so essential. Nehemiah had, he felt, his call from God; he calls it 'what God was putting into my heart to do for Jerusalem' (v. 12). That was his 'call'

---

10. During the American Revolution, George Washington would deceive his own troops about his plans to offset the frequent leaks to the British.

11. David G. Martin, *Jackson's Valley Campaign* (New York: Gallery, 1988), 25-26.

– but it must not be messed up by poor procedures. Hence secrecy. God not only calls to a task but provides savvy on how to bring it about. Which calls for praise to God only wise.

Third, Nehemiah describes **the stirring resolve of God's people** (vv. 17-18). Now the time had come to 'go public' with the people in Judah. Nehemiah told them: 'You see the disaster we are in – how Jerusalem is in ruins and its gates have been burned with fire' (v. 17a). In face of this he issues his challenge: 'Come on and let's rebuild the wall of Jerusalem, that we may no longer be a disgrace' (v. 17b). This 'pitch' Nehemiah makes already carries a subtle incentive, doesn't it? Simply the fact that he identifies with the plight of the people is telling. He is not the empire's expert talking down to them; instead, he speaks of 'we,' 'us.' He takes his stand beside them in their condition.[12]

But the overt motivation he supplies is both negative and positive. The negative is the shameful condition of Jerusalem (v. 17b). It, they, are a 'disgrace.' The word is *herpah*, which carries ideas of shame, contempt, scorn, ridicule, something to be derided. It is an unbearable state of affairs – it must be changed. Then he reports the positive incentive in verse 18a: 'And I told them of the hand of my God which had been upon me for good, and also of the words which the king had spoken to me' (RSV). So he told them of the workings of God's providence and of the king's reversal of his previous 'no build' policy. Nehemiah surely saw the latter as the outworking of the former. We have the king's permission, and we have that because, well, God conspired to bring it about that way.

Hence their vigorous response: 'And they said, "Let's get up and build" – and they strengthened their hands for the good work' (v. 18b). Of course, more will be needed than initial enthusiasm. There will have to be commitment to the long haul. But if there had not been this initial response, Project Jerusalem would have been stillborn.

I wonder if there's not something instructive for us in Nehemiah's appeal. His primary appeal was to the

---

12. F. C. Fensham, *The Books of Ezra and Nehemiah,* NICOT (Grand Rapids: Eerdmans, 1982), 167.

providence of God, what he had done, how he had ordered the circumstances, how he had maneuvered change in political policy, how he had worked 'good' for Nehemiah – and the people responded. Preachers might take note. What seems to be most effective in moving God's people? Apparently, not mere exhortation or explanation of duties, or berating for failures, or urging to 'do better'; rather, following Nehemiah's pattern, we should show them *the kind of God they have*. Perhaps this suggests *theocentric* preaching best serves and stirs Christ's flock.

Finally, Nehemiah's account underscores **the bitter animosity of God's enemies** (vv. 10, 19-20). In opposing God's people they oppose God himself.

Let us take a moment to identify these hostile agents. 'Sanballat the Horonite' is their leading spirit. He was governor of Samaria but probably considered Judah his extended sphere of influence. I could take up two pages speculating upon why he's called the 'Horonite,' but nobody really knows, so we'll drop it. He seems to have made some feint toward allegiance to Yahweh; according to the Elephantine Papyri, two of his sons were Delaiah and Shelemiah, Yahwistic names. But he was likely a syncretist. And, rather ominously, his daughter had married into the family of the high priest (13:28). Having someone with government backing come to direct affairs in Judah does not sit well with Sanballat.

Then there is 'Tobiah, the servant, the Ammonite' (vv. 10, 19). He has a Yahwistic name ('Yahweh is good'), but he is an Ammonite. Some think he was governor of Ammon (off to the east of the Jordan River). But it may be more likely that he is simply 'a Samarian official subordinate to Sanballat.'[13] It may be that he is simply Sanballat's yes-man, who has sucked up a certain flair from that association, so that he had also 'insinuated himself into the confidence of the upper classes in Jerusalem (6:17f.; 13:4f.).'[14] When Nehemiah calls him 'the *'ebed*,' he could mean it in the disparaging sense of 'slave,' rather than the more honorable sense of 'servant.' It's possible

---

13. D. J. A. Clines, *Ezra, Nehemiah, Esther*, NCBC (Grand Rapids: Eerdmans, 1984), 145.

14. ibid.

Tobiah was only Sanballat's *lackey*, who gets his clout because he is *Sanballat's* lackey.

Geshem the Arab (v. 19) is the third opponent noted, but, as it were, only noted (cf. 6:1, 6). 'Far from being a negligible alien, [he] was an even more powerful figure than his companions, though probably less earnestly committed to their cause.'[15] It appears that Geshem was 'in charge of a powerful north-Arabian confederacy of tribes that controlled vast areas from northeastern Egypt ... to northern Arabia to southern Palestine.'[16]

The animosity of Sanballat and co. came in the form of sheer malice. 'It was terribly distressing to them that a man had come to seek good for the sons of Israel' (v. 10b). *They* did not intend to seek the welfare of Israel and they didn't want anyone else doing so. The very idea repulsed them. Judah, in their view, must not thrive in any way.

Not all Sanballats live in the fifth century B.C. Come with me to the United States State Department in the 1940s. There is a man by the name of Breckinridge Long, who is in charge of the immigration and visa division. He makes immigration so difficult that the flow of refugees became a mere trickle – and that at a time, says Jay Winik, 'when Jews were being murdered first in the hundreds, then in the thousands, then in the hundreds of thousands, and then in the millions.' Applicants were subjected to terribly complex regulations. Though Long would make public statements about an open door, he circulated a secret memo indicating how the State Department could effectively stop the flow of immigrants – 'simply,' he wrote, 'advising our consuls to put every obstacle in the way and to require additional evidence and to resort to various administrative devices which would postpone and postpone and postpone the granting of visas.' So refugees despaired. One critic accused Long and associates of being an 'underground movement ... to let the Jews be killed.'[17] Here was one man in the US State Department with a malicious determination to insure the harm and doom of Jews. Sanballat *et al.* in a later edition.

---

15. Kidner, 83-84.

16. Yamauchi, EBC, 4:479.

17. Quotations from Jay Winik, *1944* (New York: Simon and Schuster, 2015), 225.

But malice must have method, and these opponents are not lacking such. Ridicule is their first resort: 'they derided us and despised us and said, "What is this thing you are doing?"' (v. 19b, RSV). Then there is innuendo – they play the political card: 'Are you rebelling against the king?' (v. 19c).

Nehemiah had an answer (v. 20); it contains three emphatic pronouns – 'He,' 'we,' 'you': 'The God of heaven, he will give us success, and we, his servants, will rise and build, and as for you – you have no portion or right or remembrance in Jerusalem.' Not even the pope could excommunicate more effectively than that!

We must, however, look beneath the surface of this opposition. It is an almost diabolical rage that drives these men. They simply cannot endure anyone coming 'to seek good for the sons of Israel' (v. 10). We are not dealing with mere human animosity, but with the serpent's seed hating the seed of the woman (cf. Gen. 3:15). It goes deeper than we may think.

In 1947 Jackie Robinson broke the 'color barrier' as the first black in US major league baseball, playing for the then Brooklyn Dodgers. It came at tremendous cost. He was the target of the nastiest verbal attacks and racial slurs. When he came to bat, pitchers would throw at him or 'dust him back' or make him drop in the dirt to avoid getting hit. Once Robinson was raging about the steady barrage of knockdown pitches he had to face. It was then that his white friend, Pee Wee Reese, the Brooklyn shortstop, had a 'word of wisdom' for him. Reese told him: 'Jack, some guys are th'owing at you because you're black and that's a terrible thing. But there are other guys, Jack, who are th'owing at you because they plain don't like you.'[18] Till then that seemed not to have occurred to Robinson. And God's people must always remember that there is something deeper behind various samples of hostility they face. 'They plain don't like you.' There is a deep-seated, relentless malice the world has for Jerusalem's citizens. So no surprises. 'And you will be hated by all on account of my name' (Mark 13:13a).

---

18. Roger Kahn, *Into My Own* (New York: St. Martin's, 2006), 107.

13

Blessed Builders
(Nehemiah 3)

Bill Veeck (rhymes with 'wreck') was the owner of several major league baseball teams in the 1940s and 1950s. He was an original character. Some would call him creative, others maddening. Every so often a team would feature a day (or night) to honor one of its outstanding players. In Cleveland it might be 'Bob Lemon Day' or 'Rocky Colavito Night,' and the honoree would be regaled with gifts. But a night watchman by the name of Joe Early wrote a letter to the *Cleveland Press* asking why ball clubs were forever having special days for baseball players who 'didn't need the loot' instead of for fans. So Veeck put on 'Good Old Joe Early Night.' Joe received several gag gifts but also a new Ford convertible, appliances, clothes, and a fine watch.[1] Which things are a hermeneutical parable. When readers and expositors come to Nehemiah they easily tend to focus on the prime human character and then use him as an example of excellence in leadership, which can lead to recitations of 'principles of effective leadership.' Well, they might say, just look at Nehemiah 3 – Nehemiah's organizing skill and ability to delegate tasks to others. But the text says nothing about that. You may think you can infer such matters from the text but the text does not press that on you. The text talks about a bunch of Joe Earlys building

---

1. Daniel Okrent and Steve Wulf, *Baseball Anecdotes* (New York: Oxford University Press, 1989), 210-11.

a wall.[2] I'm not 'putting down' Nehemiah, but we won't 'get' Nehemiah 3 unless we suppress our fixation on Nehemiah and his 'excellence in leadership.'

So much for general orientation. Now a housekeeping matter: You will find it helpful to have at hand a reconstructive sketch of Nehemiah's Jerusalem as you read this chapter. The one on the following page appears in Derek Kidner's commentary and should prove adequate.[3] The description in Nehemiah 3 starts from the NE corner and works its way counter-clockwise.

Nehemiah 3 is no bunch of dry data; this record oozes with items that should prove instructive for us. Hence these few observations.

Leaders likely make an impression. I said above that we have a bunch of 'Joe Earlys' in this record, but that does not mean there weren't men with some recognizable status. For example, Eliashib the high priest and his fellow priests (v. 1). They built the Sheep Gate on the northern part of the wall. Some seem to think that to 'build' (*banah*) may imply that previous remains had been more or less demolished, while to 'make repairs' (a form of *hazaq*, used thirty-five times in the chapter) may suggest that such sections may not have been quite so severely damaged.[4] But when both verbs are used together as in verses 13 and 15, it is hard to press a distinction. But what stands out in verse 1 is that these priests 'go at it.' Of course, this is the area near the temple, so they may have a special interest in it. Still, they

---

2. Gregory Goswell is a great help here and offers a needed corrective to the leadership craze among some expositors (*A Study Commentary on Ezra–Nehemiah* [Darlington: EP Books, 2013], 227-28, 233). For example: 'There is nothing in the content of chapter 3 that suggests that Nehemiah was responsible for organizing the local crews that worked on the forty-one different sections of the wall. The narrative is silent about Nehemiah's organizing genius (which commentators regularly praise)' (p. 227).

3. Derek Kidner, *Ezra and Nehemiah*, TOTC (Leicester: Inter-Varsity, 1979), 85. Similar is *New Bible Atlas* (Leicester: Inter-Varsity, 1985), 103. For a sketch with the names of the builders for each part, see Andrew E. Steinmann, *Ezra and Nehemiah*, CC (St. Louis, 2010), 425. This reconstruction follows a 'minimalist' view, i.e., that the repairs took in the temple mount and eastern hill but did not include the southwestern hill (the 'maximalist' view). See Steinmann's excursus (pp. 412-15) for discussion.

4. cf. Steinmann, 420.

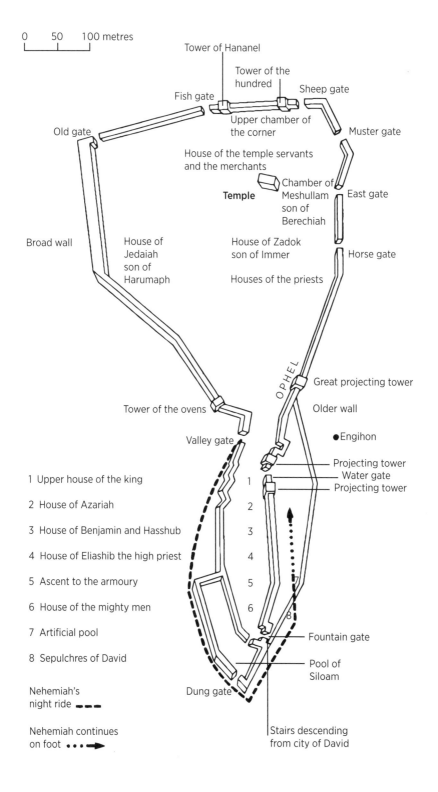

0   50   100 metres

Tower of Hananel

Tower of the hundred

Sheep gate

Fish gate

Upper chamber of the corner

Muster gate

Old gate

House of the temple servants and the merchants

Chamber of Meshullam son of Berechiah

East gate

Temple

Broad wall

House of Jedaiah son of Harumaph

House of Zadok son of Immer

Horse gate

Houses of the priests

OPHEL

Great projecting tower

Older wall

Tower of the ovens

●Engihon

Valley gate

Projecting tower

Water gate

Projecting tower

1 Upper house of the king

2 House of Azariah

3 House of Benjamin and Hasshub

4 House of Eliashib the high priest

5 Ascent to the armoury

6 House of the mighty men

7 Artificial pool

8 Sepulchres of David

Nehemiah's night ride ▬ ▬ ▬

Nehemiah continues on foot • • • ➤

Fountain gate

Pool of Siloam

Dung gate

Stairs descending from city of David

didn't flash any 'clergy exemption' cards. They didn't think their priesthood somehow constituted them immune to the work. One would think that would favorably impress the rest of the laborers.

Not all of the leader-types shared the priests' initiative. Next to Zadok's group (v. 4) some men from Tekoa repaired (v. 5). Tekoa was the prophet Amos' hometown (Amos 1:1), ten miles south of Jerusalem. But not everybody from Tekoa was pro-wall: 'but their nobles did not bring their neck into the service of their lords' (v. 5b). That's rather literal. The image is of an animal, like an ox, submitting its neck to a yoke in order to do farm work. That last word could be 'lords,' referring perhaps to Jerusalem leadership or to the overseers of the Tekoa contingent, or it could be rendered 'Lord,' the ultimate master. In any case some of the upper-mucks in Tekoa were not about to lower themselves to labor on the wall project. Why they were opposed to it is ultimately a matter of conjecture. We don't know if it was arrogance or antagonism, or both. Thankfully, there were others of some status who did not fight shy of wall labor – I think of those men who apparently were district administrators, over half of Jerusalem (two of them, vv. 9, 12), over Beth-hakkerem (perhaps three miles SSW of Jerusalem, v. 14), Mizpah (seven miles NNW of Jerusalem, v. 15), half of Beth-zur (four-plus miles N of Hebron, v. 16), over half of Keilah (two of them, vv. 17-18; eighteen miles SW of Jerusalem). Whatever level of respect and responsibility these men had did not keep them from the grunt work of clearing rubbish, hauling rock, and reconstructing gates.

Such 'stooping' usually impresses people. During the London 'Blitz' in 1940, Winston Churchill arrived in the East End to view the damage and to see survivors. One might think folks would resent him since he could not prevent such devastation. But that was not the case. Here was a large crowd at the air raid shelter where forty people had been killed. No sooner had Churchill emerged from the car than the people mobbed him. 'Good old Winnie,' some shouted; others: 'We thought you'd come and see us.' Churchill went regularly to the East End during the blitz to boost morale. Hitler, his counterpart in Germany, never visited bomb-sites but would drive past with curtains drawn in his Mercedes-Benz.[5] Unlike Nehemiah 3, Churchill's visits didn't involve manual labor, but the principle is similar: having a leader standing among their rubble inclines them to think that it – and they – matter to him. And we know the ultimate example of this sort of thing appears in Philippians 2:5-11.

Secondly, we can see **the motive of personal interest** operating in these repairs. According to Yamauchi, some forty-one parties are listed as reconstructing forty-two sections. If re-building was confined to the eastern hill (the 'minimalist' view), the circuit would have been about two miles and would have enclosed about ninety acres.[6] Now among the builders are the likes of Jehaiah, Benjamin and Hasshub, Azariah, some priests, Zadok, and Meshullam, all of whom are said to have repaired the wall next to their houses or quarters (vv. 10, 23 [twice], 28, 29, 30). Nothing wrong with that. Not all builders could have such assignments, but clearly, where possible, it was a counsel of wisdom. They would surely perform quality repairs if it was part of the defense of their own homes. In 1948 when the Jewish sector of Jerusalem was being slowly strangled by an Arab cordon, there was yet a window of time to get the women and children to the coast and away from besieged Jerusalem. Dov Joseph, a Canadian lawyer in charge of provisioning Jewish Jerusalem, refused to allow the evacuation. He reasoned that Jewish men would fight harder to defend their section of Jerusalem if they knew the lives of their wives and children depended on their tenacity and bravery. They didn't need to be told what would happen to their families if the Arabs overran their positions. Personal interest can be quite a motivator, and was, sometimes, in Nehemiah's Jerusalem.

One can also see in this record **the evidence and encouragement of zeal**. What if you were Shallum the son of Hallohesh (v. 12)? Apparently he had no sons, no muscled males to help him in repairs. That didn't deter him. He had daughters. Who knows how many? Maybe three or four?

---

5. See Andrew Roberts, *Churchill: Walking with Destiny* (New York: Viking, 2018), 593.

6. EBC, 4:480.

They could do construction work. Did they put up a small sign at the base of their section: 'Year 445, Shallum and girls'?

Then there were those who shouldered double duty. Meremoth son of Uriah repaired two sections (vv. 4, 21), as did Meshullam son of Berechiah (vv. 4, 30). Tekoa had its malcontents (v. 5b), but their main work crew took on double duty also (vv. 5a, 27). And, of course, that quite a number of workers came from towns beyond Jerusalem (e.g., vv. 5, 7, 13, 14, 15, 16, 17, 19, 27) indicates an earnest commitment on their part to see Jerusalem established as the fortress it should be. Such zeal seemed to please and encourage Nehemiah – at least that idea seems to lurk behind his comment in 4:6, 'the people had a mind to work.'

We should also observe that the whole wall project is primarily **the achievement of non-professionals.** In 1972, in war-ravaged Bangladesh, a medical missionary, Dr Viggo Olsen, had undertaken the responsibility of building 4,000 homes. In his daily Bible reading he had just finished Ezra and was beginning Nehemiah. He speaks of the morning when he was reading 'the tedious third chapter of Nehemiah.' 'I was struck,' he says, 'that no expert builders were listed in the "Holy Land Brigade"; there were priests, priests' helpers, goldsmiths, perfume-makers, and women, but no expert builders or carpenters were named.'[7] Nehemiah 3 supplied incentive for Olsen and his crews to finish 4,000 homes in seven weeks.

But that is so typical of Israel's God, isn't it? He seems to have a certain bias toward ordinary servants. That's why, as we read our Bibles, we keep running into people like Jonathan's armor-bearer (1 Sam. 14:7), and Abigail's informant (1 Sam. 25:14), and Jehosheba (2 Kings 11:1-2), and Ebedmelech (Jer. 38:7-9), and Shecaniah (Ezra 10:2!), and Paul's nephew (Acts 23:16), and Epaphroditus (Phil. 2:25-30), and Onesiphorus (2 Tim. 1:16-18). Isn't this matter a healthy reminder in a day when the church is sometimes so a-gawk over 'competence' and professional skills?

It is true, we cannot follow the turf exactly at every point, cannot locate every spot in Nehemiah's Jerusalem

---

7. Cited in Donald K. Campbell, *Nehemiah: Man in Charge* (Wheaton, IL: Victor, 1979), 34.

precisely. And it's true that Nehemiah 3 is not as stirring and scintillating as many Old Testament narratives. Yet the names here constitute a *roll of honor* of Yahweh's workers – in place to be remembered. Names matter. That's why they are here in Nehemiah 3. Maybe few will remember them. But Jesus surely will. Anyone who doesn't forget cold cups of water (Matt. 10:42) will surely remember these men and women.

14

Threats against God's Work
(Nehemiah 4)

We can break down Nehemiah 4 into three main sections, each of which begins with Sanballat and co. or the Jews' enemies 'hearing' (vv. 1, 7, 15) of the work or progress on the wall; hence verses 1-6, 7-14, and 15-23 are our divisions.[1] Moreover, at the end or near the end of each section one meets with some sort of an expression of faith (note vv. 4-5, 14, 20). John Newton's hymn provides us with a suitable rubric for all of chapters 4–6: 'through many dangers, toils, and snares.' Chapter 4 simply reports the first wave of these.

First, in verses 1-6, Nehemiah tells us of **ridicule – and lethal prayer**. Sanballat wasted no time pondering a retort:

> When Sanballat heard that we were building the wall, it burned him up, he was terribly infuriated, and mocked the Jews. So he said before his cohorts and the army of Samaria, 'What are these pathetic Jews doing? Will they do it (all) by themselves? Will they sacrifice? Will they finish in a day? Will they revive the stones from piles of rubble––burned as they are?' (vv. 1-2).

Scorn often works like this. Like the chief priests and scribes who mocked Jesus 'to one another' (Mark 15:31-32), Sanballat does not address the Jews directly but his cronies *about* the Jews.

---

1. Verses 1-6 in the English text are included as the final section of chapter 3 in the Hebrew text; but our exposition will follow the versification of most English translations.

123

Even though he had an armed Samarian contingent with him (perhaps to intimidate), there is a certain helplessness about his mockery. It's as if that's all he could do. Nehemiah did, after all, have official permission from the king, with accompanying documents, and that doubtless frustrated Sanballat no end.[2]

Yet derision and ridicule are part of their arsenal. Tobiah the Ammonite, like the yes-man he was, added his one-liner: 'If a fox would go up on what they're building, he would burst open their stone wall' (v. 3). Naturally, Tobiah is loopy; he exaggerates; no fox will imperil a wall nine feet thick.[3] But the opposition begins here, with ridicule.

How, then, does one react to this? With a few hard-hitting one-liners from one's mental file? No, but with *devastating prayer:*

> Hear, our God, for we have been despised, and return their ridicule on their heads, and assign them for plunder in a land where they are captive. And don't cover over their guilt, and don't let their sin be wiped out before you, for they have infuriated (you?) before the builders (vv. 4-5).

There is some question about the last line, but Nehemiah's prayer doesn't lack clarity. If Sanballat 'heard' (v. 1), now Yahweh will 'hear' (v. 4).

Nothing tentative about this prayer. He asks that their guilt not be covered nor their sin erased. Someone might want to ask Nehemiah, 'But what if they repent?' But Nehemiah is not considering contingencies here. Why stifle prayer with a bunch of 'what ifs'? It is a frightening prayer. Be careful about mocking God's servants – that mockery may be met with brutal prayer. Only too late can we tell Sanballat: beware of prayer. That is what Nehemiah does here – he does not unload on the mockers; he unloads to God about the mockers. Would that we were so programmed to respond that way.

How are we to view Nehemiah's prayer here? It makes some believers and interpreters nervous; they seem to sense it sounds contradictory to New Testament teaching and 'the

---

2. F. C. Fensham, *The Books of Ezra and Nehemiah*, NICOT (Grand Rapids: Eerdmans, 1982), 180.

3. cf. Edwin M. Yamauchi, *Persia and the Bible* (Grand Rapids: Baker, 1990), 270.

spirit of Jesus' (seldom defined), and so unworthy of 'New Testament Christians.' But before anyone jumps all over Nehemiah, keep the following observations in mind ...

1. It is a prayer for justice, for judgment against sin. As such, it is a prayer for *God* to act; Nehemiah is not presuming to take vengeance into his own hands; he commits that to God, which is exactly what Romans 12 instructs us to do.

2. The prayer presupposes that the project in question is the work of God; hence to mock it or those doing it is to assault the honor of God.

3. These are not *personal* enemies (as those, for example, Jesus speaks of in Matthew 5:43f.) but enemies of God's kingdom.

4. There is no indication that Sanballat, Tobiah *et al.* repented or sought repentance, and so considerations like those in Matthew 18:21-22 do not apply (sentimentalists sometimes seem to expect such).[4]

Though Nehemiah's is quite a vigorous prayer, we may still regard it as a weak response. Respond with prayer? But it's hardly a weak response. It's the proper – and effective – resort for God's people facing wrong (Exod. 22:22-23; Deut. 15:9; 24:15). Enemies of Jesus' people won't pay attention, but we should still warn them: beware of prayer.

Then what? 'So we built the wall' (v. 6a). No one has said it as well as Derek Kidner:

> [T]he sturdy simplicity of that statement, and of the behaviour it records, makes Sanballat and his friends suddenly appear rather small and shrill, dwarfed by the faith, unity and energy of the weak.[5]

They simply press on with what they were called to do.

In the second segment we meet with **intimidation – and faithful vigilance** (vv. 7-14). Part of the intimidation comes

---

4. Sometimes Jesus' teaching is sentimentalized; on Luke 6:27-30, for example, see my *Luke 1–13* (Ross-shire: Christian Focus, 2021), 115-17.

5. *Ezra and Nehemiah*, TOTC (Leicester: Inter-Varsity, 1979), 91.

simply from the geographical vicious circle Jerusalem faced. Verse 7 ticks off the locations: Sanballat to the north, Arabs to the south, Ammonites to the east, and Ashdod to the west. Judah was surrounded. The placement of her enemies was intimidation enough.

Sanballat had been 'burned up' over this Wall Restoration Project (v. 1), but now that progress was being made and 'the gaps were being closed' (HCSB), he and his cronies were *really* burned up' (last of v. 7). So they threatened an armed assault to throw Jerusalem into confusion and chaos (v. 8). One might wonder how they could dare do that since Nehemiah had government approval for this task. But Sanballat may have reasoned that Susa was a long ways off and that 'here is here' and that interim measures might be taken without causing too many ripples with the central government. For example, Sanballat may have intended a sort of reconnaissance-in-force that would scare the liver out of the Jews, so that they would terminate their efforts.

Verse 9 shows how the builders faced the latest threat: 'So we prayed to our God and set up a guard against them.' Note the telling theology here. They avoid both the error of self-reliance and that of lazy inertia. They avoid both the sin of panic and the sin of paralysis. This combination of faith *and* preparedness saves them from frivolity (the let-go-and-let-God attitude) and idolatry (all depends on our own efforts).

This matter, however, is only one part of the difficulty. Verses 10-12 highlight the *troubling talk* making the rounds. Three times in these verses someone is saying something and none of it encouraging. In the end it only reinforces the intimidation.

The first down-note comes from the builders themselves, expressing their own discouragement over the task (v. 10). Their words seem to have a cadence to them; the text is hard to 'Englishfy' but perhaps we can catch the tone in the paraphrase of *The Message:*

> The builders are pooped,
> the rubbish piles up;
> We're in over our heads,
> we can't build this wall.

As McConville reminds us, this rubbish was not 'the beer can variety' but heavy rubble; especially on the eastern slopes there had been extensive collapse of houses and walls; the terrain, except on the north, was very steep; and the arduous business of heaving and exposing and finding usable material among it all was terribly wearisome.[6] Utter fatigue takes its toll. Some suggest that this chant might have been something like the spirituals of, e.g., nineteenth-century slaves, which for all the negative tone nevertheless kept them going.[7] However, the builders were likely affected by the fresh threat in verses 7-9, and this 'singing the blues' was their despairing response.

But the trouble is more direct – their adversaries speak in verse 11, renewing their threat: 'they will never know and they will never see until we come among them and kill them and put a stop to the work.' If you were in Jerusalem, you could not dismiss this as mere saber-rattling; it sounds life-threatening; it sounds *deadly* serious.

Then there is the talk of verse 12. The last part of the verse is very difficult. But it seems as though the Jews who are talking here have been listening to the propaganda of the Jews' enemies. The Jews who come to Nehemiah and associates are those who 'live beside them.' I assume this means that these Jews live beside/among the Jews' enemies in the countryside and towns in Judah. These Jews kept saying something repeatedly (lit., 'ten times'); then the text has this phrase, 'from all places.' I prefer to take this as a brief parenthesis, i.e., that these Jews came from all places in Judah and their message was, 'You must return to us.' That is, these Jews who may be from outlying towns, like Tekoa or Keilah, for example, are fearful for their own security and want their men who are working in Jerusalem to come home and provide more protection for their home folks – probably because Sanballat's goons have made threats against these outlying Jewish settlements. It's the propaganda of Sanballat's agents that scares these Jewish communities and so eggs them to badger the Jerusalem workers to come home. Such fears and rumors would only demoralize the workers all the more. Take all this talk in verses 10-12 together and

---

6. J. G. McConville, *Ezra, Nehemiah, and Esther*, Daily Study Bible (Philadelphia: Westminster, 1985), 91.

7. McConville, 92.

one needs little imagination to sense the withering effect it would have.

So much for the 'intimidation.' In verses 13-14 we see the 'faithful vigilance' in the face of it. These verses are a sort of re-take of verse 9. Nehemiah's immediate preparation consists of placing armed people in the most vulnerable portions of the rebuilding, sporting swords, spears, and bows (v. 13). Swords were used in close combat, spears for stabbing and thrusting at close range, and bows for long range; if it was a composite bow, it had a range of 700 yards, accurate at 300–400.[8] All this quietly said to Sanballat's thugs, 'We're ready for you.'

Yet Nehemiah did not live by weapons alone. One sees that in verse 14 in his 'Remember-the-Lord' speech. He tells his people, 'Don't be afraid of them; remember the great and fearful Lord and fight for your brothers, your sons, and your daughters, your wives and your homes.' Nehemiah's words are really just a clone of the 'Onward-Israeli-soldiers' speech the priests were to give Israel when facing a formidable enemy (Deut. 20:1-4). This immediate preparation was effective (v. 15a), at least for the moment.

What we must be careful to see is the 'both-and' component in Nehemiah's efforts. We saw it in verse 9, and now again in verses 13-14. There is trust in the Lord (v. 14) *and* human vigilance (v. 13). We are often tempted to omit one or the other, or play one off against the other. But Nehemiah's nexus consists of both: 'Remember the Lord … and fight!'

Moe Berg was a major league baseball catcher with the Chicago White Sox, knew several languages, including Sanskrit, and had graduated from Columbia Law School. He was also a spy. During 1934 Berg went with a team of all-stars (that included Babe Ruth and Lou Gehrig) on a baseball tour to Japan. Berg delivered the welcoming speech in Japanese – he also addressed the Japanese legislature. Pretending illness one day, he filled the time by taking reconnaissance photographs of Tokyo for the US State Department. Berg's pictures were used in World War II in preparation for General

---

8. Fensham, 186, drawing on Yadin.

Jimmy Doolittle's bombers.[9] *We* probably don't associate the categories of professional athlete and government spy with each other, but for Moe Berg they seemed perfectly compatible. Not one or the other, but both. So with any one of Nehemiah's men: he had a great and fearful Lord *and* he lugged a sword while working on the wall. The principle involved has repeated applications in the circumstances of Christian believers.

The third segment of our text focuses on **frustration – and an ongoing regimen** (vv. 15-23). The frustration belongs to the Jews' enemies: 'Now when our enemies heard that it was known to us and that God had frustrated their scheme, then all of us returned to the wall, each to his work' (v. 15). The 'it' that was known was their foes' plan to attack (cf. vv. 8, 11). Sanballat may have been dumbfounded when Nehemiah and his men went into preparedness mode. Perhaps they may not have counted on these Jews having the initiative and gumption to go 'military' on them. So wall work went on – and so did wariness. After all, one doesn't trust snakes.

Yet Nehemiah instituted some new measures, at least for the interim. He still held the same confidence – 'Our God [emphatic] will fight for us' (v. 20b), but put in place more defensive procedures. There seem to be several groups that figure in Nehemiah's revised building plan. Nehemiah himself had a contingent of servants who did wall work – half of them worked on the wall while half held weapons in readiness (v. 16a). Nehemiah's own entourage was itself a model of how the work should go on. The leaders or officials in verse 16b may have been on permanent guard duty. Then there were the load-luggers (v. 17), who would carry loads and their weapons at the same time. There were the builders (v. 18), each with his sword strapped on. And there was an alarm system in place (vv. 18b-20).

Nor was this all. Nehemiah demanded that workers from outside Jerusalem no longer go home at night (v. 22). No more commuting! They were to stay in Jerusalem to help with guard duty. Who knows how that requirement was

---

9. Daniel Okrent and Steve Wulf, *Baseball Anecdotes* (New York: Oxford, 1989), 94-95.

received? But, even if it was found uncongenial, no one could say Nehemiah and his men were opting out of the severe regimen – they never seemed to be off duty at all (v. 23).[10] And in all of this there was yet steady progress: 'And so we worked on' (v. 21a, NJPS).

Their enemies had been stymied. But far from letting down his guard, Nehemiah had instituted even more readiness measures. I'm not trying to 'spiritualize' the text but only want to point out that though it seems like Jerusalem wall-building is a long way from where we live, the real concern of the text is the same. It's behind Jesus' Word to us: 'Watch and pray that you may not enter into temptation' (Matt. 26:41, RSV). You simply must *never* let your guard down.

As I look back over Nehemiah 4, it reminds me of something I see most every Tuesday morning, while it's still dark. That's when I throw the big, black plastic bags of household garbage into the back of my pick-up to dispose of them at our friendly dump and re-cycle center. On my way, at a particular intersection on the edge of town, there is a convenience store that also sells Citgo gasoline. Above the gas pumps there's that protective canopy in which there are six bright lights that illuminate the pump area. One of those lights blinks, all the time, rapidly and relentlessly. Five of the lights are normal, this one is nervous. The effect is similar to a tubular fluorescent bulb in one's home when its lifespan is up and it only pulses or blinks. I would think Citgo fuel purchasers would go mad as they filled their tanks. I don't know if it's a ballast or what the trouble is, but it's *never been fixed*. I've gone by there for years and that one-in-six light goes on blinking. Which is a parable of Jerusalem's troubles in Nehemiah 4. They simply go on and on. The enemies of Christ's people never stop their assaults. They've a hatred that can't stop hating. Jesus, as always, was right (Mark 13:13).

---

10. The last of verse 23 is a teaser. Literally, it reads: 'each his weapon the water(s).' It may mean each man took his weapon with him even when he went to drink or to wash. But it is so enigmatic that one can't be sure.

15

Folly among God's People
(Nehemiah 5)

It was 1957. Hank Aaron was returning to his home turf near Mobile, Alabama. Mobile had arranged a Hank Aaron Day. Well, he was an all-star outfielder for the (then) Milwaukee Braves and they had just won major league baseball's World Series. A band met his family at the train station and struck up its numbers. The mayor gave him the key to the city. A rather enjoyable bit of hoopla. However, Hank had been invited to speak at one of the white service clubs in town. He asked if he could bring his father with him. After hemming and hawing, they refused his request. Apparently, it was fine to have a black all-star speaking to them, but they couldn't have his black daddy sitting among all these pristine white fellows. So, naturally, Hank turned down the 'opportunity.'[1] That is a pattern frequently repeated: a measure of delight or progress and then a blot falls over the whole affair. It is the pattern one sees in Nehemiah 4–5: we see such progress and perseverance in rebuilding the wall (ch. 4), only then to hear the outcry and distress of Jews who are being bled dry by their own people (ch. 5). Nehemiah 5 is the blot on the Jerusalem urban renewal project. External assault was the fear in chapter 4; in chapter 5 the danger arises from internal dispute.

---

1. Henry Aaron, with Lonnie Wheeler, *I Had a Hammer* (New York: HarperCollins, 1991), 132-33.

Nehemiah 5 broadly falls into two sections, verses 1-13 and 14-19, but, for our purposes, I want to take it in three divisions, the first of which can be called: **a dire trouble** (vv. 1-5).

Here then is a huge protest by men and their wives with reference to 'their brothers, the Jews' (v. 1). It's an 'internal' problem and a bit multi-faceted. In the thrice-occurring 'there were those saying' in verses 2, 3, and 4, there seem to be at least three groups, each with something of its own difficulty.[2] The *first group* that spoke up consisted of families who may have owned no land and yet had to eat; it may be that having to take time to work on the wall diminished their time and ability to earn wages (v. 2). We must realize that the Red Cross did not feed Jerusalem's workers gratis from several feeding stations.

The *second group* consisted of those who were mortgaging their land, farms, and/or homes in order to get food, and these folks would lose this security completely if they could not pay their debts with proceeds from the annual harvest (v. 3). And harvest did not look promising given the famine (v. 3b). Then the *third group* consisted of those having to borrow, again with fields and vineyards as collateral, in order to pay the king's taxes (vv. 4-5). They had to sell some of their family members into debt-slavery because of this hardship.

A brief tangent on 'the king's tax' (v. 4) may be useful. The Persian king collected about twenty million darics a year in taxes. (A daric equaled the price of an ox or a month's wages for a soldier.) Little of this was returned to the satrapies. Usual practice was to melt down the gold and silver and stash it away as bullion. At Susa alone Alexander the Great found 9,000 talents of coined gold (*c.* 270 tons) and 40,000 talents of silver (*c.* 1,200 tons) stored up as bullion. M. Dandamayev (cited by Yamauchi) has written: 'Documents from Babylonia show that many inhabitants of this satrapy too had to mortgage their fields and orchards to get silver for the payment of taxes to the king. In many cases they were unable to redeem their property, and became landless hired laborers; sometimes they were compelled to give away their children into slavery.'

---

2. See, e.g., H. G. M. Williamson, 'Nehemiah,' in *New Bible Commentary*, 4th. ed. (Leicester: Inter-Varsity, 1994), 436.

And interest rates were high. They rose from 20 per cent in the time of Cyrus and Cambyses to 40–50 per cent at the end of the fifth century. In short, the Persians were rather lenient with subject peoples in religious matters but taxed the socks off of them.[3]

Here in Nehemiah 5, however, the problem was probably not interest or usury (much as some translations like RSV and NIV would have it) but debt-slavery – with well-off Jews playing loan sharks and then possessing the pledge and collateral that needier Jews put up when the latter were unable to pay the principal.[4] One can sense the frustration of those mired in debt in verse 5: they can't do anything to buy back their children from debt-slavery because 'all their produce from the land goes straight to the creditors' (whether those creditors had actually taken possession of the property or not).[5] The lid was on the box; there was no way they could get ahead.

The crying shame is that the profiteers were fellow Jews (vv. 1, 7). There was trouble enough in Jerusalem from external enemies (chapters 4 and 6); yet in the midst of that these profiteers are undercutting and destroying their own people. It's about as brilliant as what we hear of in the much later Roman sack of Jerusalem in A.D. 70. When Titus was moving in on Jerusalem, there were three factions among the Jews. One had control of the upper city and a large part of the lower city; one dominated the temple mount, and another the inner forecourt of the temple. All three were locked in constant fighting among themselves – the city was an unceasing battlefield. Then, in face of the Roman siege, they sent up in flames the huge stores of grain in the city to prevent the other factions from having access to it. Blatant stupidity.[6]

---

3. For all this, see Yamauchi, EBC, 4:401-2, 495-96; and Mervin Breneman, *Ezra, Nehemiah, Esther*, NAC (n.p.: Broadman & Holman, 1993), 201; cf. also A. T. Olmstead, *History of the Persian Empire* (Chicago: U. of Chicago, 1948), 297-99.

4. See NIDOTTE, 3:178; and Gregory Goswell, *A Study Commentary on Ezra–Nehemiah* (Darlington: EP Books, 2013), 249-50.

5. D. J. A. Clines, *Ezra, Nehemiah, Esther*, NCBC (Grand Rapids: Eerdmans, 1984), 167.

6. Emil Schurer, *The History of the Jewish People in the Age of Jesus Christ (175 B.C.–A.D. 135)*, rev. ed., G. Vermes and F. Millar, eds. (Edinburgh: T. and T. Clark, 1973), vol. 1:501.

There is something of that here in Nehemiah: with surrounding enemies salivating to attack them, they afford themselves the luxury of Jews oppressing fellow Jews. It was not only foolish, it was heartless and, naturally, disappointing. An episode from American history may supply a partial parallel (with apologies to British readers, who may think otherwise).

In the 'War of 1812,' actually about 1814, Sir George Prevost's troops, about 18,000 redcoats, began moving down Lake Champlain. They would soon have been suffering from famine, except that they had 'friendly enemies' to the south. Two thirds of Prevost's army were supplied by American contractors, mainly from Vermont and New York. So these northeastern American states were funneling beef to the British – essentially warring against their own government and troops. And why? Profits. The Brits paid well.[7] They were going against 'their own people.'

This last is the problem in Nehemiah 5. And in terms of a passing application I would simply point out that it shows how *disappointing* God's covenant people can be.[8] The same holds true to this day, with regard to the church. I don't want to bad-mouth the church – all sorts of others are always doing so. But the fact remains that it's among the officially covenant people that you run into questionable ethics, lack of discernment, frivolous interests, petty disputes, major moral failures, and so on. The church ought not to be like that; but sometimes it is. I don't want to be cynical about the church, nor make you cynical. But, if anything, Nehemiah 5 should warn us not to expect too much. Maybe we are on the edge of a paradox here: recognizing that the church is often disappointing may save you from being *too* disappointed with the church.

Let us move on to verses 6-13. Here the distress and clamor Nehemiah faces leads to **a forceful solution**. He candidly says, 'I was really burned up when I heard their outcry' (v. 6). But

---

7. Robert Leckie, *The Wars of America*, 2 vols. (New York: Harper & Row, 1968), 1:292.

8. This is a sort of 'broad principle' application. Some would probably prefer to read a rip-roaring 'social justice' application. All interpreters would do well to read Gary R. Williams, 'Contextual Influences in Readings of Nehemiah 5: A Case Study,' *Tyndale Bulletin* 53.1 (2002): 57-74, which, among other things, shows that applications interpreters make from Nehemiah 5 often say more about the interpreter than the text.

his anger did not short circuit careful thought (v. 7a), which led him to bring charges against the main perpetrators before a public assembly (v. 7b).

The primary offense, again, was probably not exacting interest (as, e.g., in ESV in v. 7) but imposing a claim for repayment of debt, as NJPS has it: 'Are you pressing claims on loans made to your brothers?' [Answer: Yes, you are.] Apparently, in recent times some destitute Jews had been sold to surrounding peoples, and Nehemiah and co. had redeemed them, purchased them back (v. 8a). But what were these loan sharks who sold fellow Jews like that (v. 8b) trying to do?

Were they trying to add to Nehemiah's *ad hoc* buy-back program? These fellows were all heart![9] Nehemiah exposed and shamed these men in front of the whole assembly (v. 8).

Now Nehemiah candidly admits that he and his colleagues had also made loans of money and grain (v. 10a). He does *not* say that he pressured his debtors with dire threats to pay up – and we must assume that he did not. However, he says that the whole loan apparatus must be done away with: 'Let us now abandon this practice of loans' (v. 10b, Williamson). A hard-pressed people must be 'cut some slack.' Nehemiah's *order* (v. 11) is for the profiteers to return collateral they had sucked up, as well as 'surcharges' they had demanded.[10] Verse 11 may require a 'double' sort of restoration: not only the *means* of production (fields, vineyards, olive groves, houses) but also interim *provisions* (grain, wine, oil) for immediate need.[11]

---

9. See Derek Kidner, *Ezra and Nehemiah*, TOTC (Leicester: Inter-Varsity, 1979), 96. Note also Stephen S. Short, 'Nehemiah,' in *The New Layman's Bible Commentary* (Grand Rapids: Zondervan, 1979), 539: Nehemiah 'recalled to them that his own practice had been the very opposite of their own, and that whenever he had seen Jewish slaves offered for sale in a Gentile market-place, he would pay the ransom price and give them their liberty. But these Jewish nobles, on occasion, in order to make money, would sell poverty-stricken fellow-countrymen of theirs to heathen masters in the knowledge that Nehemiah, seeing their plight, would buy them back.'

10. Part of what was to be returned was, literally, 'a hundredth of the silver/ money,' and there is even some dispute about that 'literal' translation. No one seems to know for sure what this means; it may allude to some interest charge.

11. Don't get on your horse and gallop off to use Nehemiah's measures here as justification for some program for 'restoring economic equality.' Nehemiah's regimen was imposed to meet an urgent crisis at a particular hour. It was not necessarily intended, beyond general principles, to serve as an ongoing, continuing

The moneylenders give their *consent* to Nehemiah's order (v. 12a), yet Nehemiah presses for a bit more 'clout' and so calls the priests to administer an *oath* (v. 12b) in the matter – after which Nehemiah graphically depicted the *curse* (v. 13) that would overtake any who reneged on their obligation.

Seems like Nehemiah's response could be taken as heavy-handed, domineering, abrupt, brash. It *was* a forceful solution. But before you are tempted to throw eggs at Nehemiah, you must understand how critical the situation was. Sometimes one can't take time to form a committee. Once in our church building in Baltimore a bat (the building occasionally had bat problems) began swooping around in my study, a room maybe twelve feet by twenty-five at most. Hard to ignore. I got a broom and knocked it down in flight, then beat it to death on the carpet (for which one of the readers of my 1 Kings commentary berated me – since he had never had a bat invade his study). Bats should know that a pastor's study is verboten turf. But you can't sit around and pretend there's nothing wrong. You don't call the elders or deacons. You have to deal with it. And that's what Nehemiah did here – effectively.

Yet Nehemiah did not simply bludgeon his way through this mess. His was a reasoned and principled approach. You can catch it in verse 9: 'This thing,' he said, 'which you are doing is not good; should you not walk in the fear of our God because of the scorn of the nations, our enemies?' There is the basis of biblical ethics: the fear of God. If you fear God, you will not distress and destroy people. If you fear God, you will not try to crush people. This is not the last we will hear of this 'fear.'

---

program. Aside from this stricture, however, one can only applaud Christ's servants in our own day who maintain ministries that give economic help to the Lord's people. There are a number of these. One is spearheaded by Wyatt George, a personal friend, which provides micro-loans to needy believers in Uganda. Donors contribute funds to the Tentmaker Project, which is under the oversight of a local Presbyterian church in Uganda. Loan candidates are instructed in biblical business, economic, and stewardship principles. Some are then selected for loans – it may be for setting up a piggery, or chicken farm, or perhaps managing an apartment complex. After they begin to make a profit in their business, they begin to pay back the loan, which funds are then used to extend loans to others. Loan payback is, I believe, at something like 90 per cent. My reason for the proviso at the beginning of this note is to head off any who want to politicize Nehemiah and make him a John-the-Baptist figure for Karl Marx.

Thirdly, verses 14-19 provide us with **a personal defense** from Nehemiah. This section is something like an extract from Nehemiah's diary. It interrupts, as it were, the narrative flow, since he speaks of his whole twelve-year tenure as governor and not merely of the turmoil just addressed. But he places this segment here to set forth a *positive sample* of his walking in the fear of God (v. 15) over against the heartlessness of the profiteering Jews in verses 1-13.

Nehemiah strikes certain keynotes in his 'defense.' One we can call *relinquishment*. Nehemiah had certain rights by virtue of his position as the appointed governor – a food allowance, for example (v. 14); and former governors had burdened the people to provide those funds (v. 15). Nehemiah voluntarily gave that up. And yet he faced the cost of providing food for the constant flow of guests and visitors to his daily table, a cost he absorbed out of his own private funds (vv. 17-18). He also highlights his *focus* (v. 16): he held so tenaciously to the task of rebuilding the wall that secondary activities, like purchasing land, never occupied him. Moreover, his servants were so focused as well (v. 16b). Nor does he neglect to mention his *motives*. In verse 15b he notes that even the servants of former governors 'lorded it over' the people, 'but I [emphatic] did not do that because of the fear of God.' Here is concern for the people along with 'the fear of God.' In the last of verse 18 he also notes his consideration for the people: he didn't demand his rightful food allowance because it would be too much for the people to bear. Fear of the Lord and compassion for the people were his driving motives. Reverence for God and mercy for people motivated this kind of self-sacrificing, non-oppressive leadership. Would that the wheelers and dealers of verse 9 had been driven by the same motives!

One can almost guess that someone is going to gripe about this. Some will object that Nehemiah is tooting his own horn, strutting his own righteousness. But he's not. He's only demonstrating his integrity. He's not flaunting some sinless perfection. He is simply being Paul before Paul. Check out the apostle's argument in 1 Thessalonians 2. Paul tells those believers that they could be sure he and his associates were not just another band of religious charlatans salivating over cash flow for their 'ministry.' No, Paul took no support from these people; rather, he worked at his trade to support himself (v. 9) as he gave the gospel to them. That's the thrust of Nehemiah's defense. He is not advertising his self-righteousness but demonstrating his sincerity. Perfectly proper.

All of which leads to a perfectly proper prayer: 'Remember me, O my God, for good, in view of all I have done for this people' (v. 19). Where does one look for reward? You don't expect it from people – you seek it from God, as this prayer in verse 19 does. It's as if Nehemiah knows the Savior of Matthew 10:42 and the God of Hebrews 6:10.

16

Stratagems against God's Servant
(Nehemiah 6)

W e who live in nations with freedom of speech and freedom of the press are used to hearing our most visible leaders, whether prime minister or president, come under verbal attack. He or she may be criticized for policies, lampooned for follies, vilified for failures. Not that such leaders are necessarily solely responsible, but, since they are 'up front,' they receive the brunt of the backlash. Antagonism for projects or programs seems to land on the person. That's something of what we find in Nehemiah 6. Here the opposition aims not so much at the wall project as in Nehemiah 4 but at Nehemiah himself, seeking to intimidate, spook, or discredit him. Or, even to eliminate him (cf. v. 2). Note the dominant emphasis on *fear* (vv. 9, 13, 14, 19) throughout the chapter, which easily breaks down into three segments (vv. 1-9, 10-14, 15-19).[1]

The first attempt against Nehemiah centers on **liquidation— and slander** (vv. 1-9). There had been substantial progress on the wall—no broken-down places were left in it (v. 1). Sanballat and Geshem wanted a 'consultation' (v. 2). Perhaps they hyped their proposal with 'Why don't we try to settle this via diplomacy?' Or they may have pitched nonsense like 'We're really not as far apart as may appear.' Maybe they

---

1. H. G. M. Williamson, *Ezra, Nehemiah*, WBC (Waco: Word, 1985), 251; Gregory Goswell, *A Study Commentary on Ezra–Nehemiah* (Darlington: EP Books, 2013), 262.

could pow-wow on the plain of Ono, 'neutral' territory, about twenty-seven miles northwest of Jerusalem (not far from modern Israel's airport just east of Tel Aviv). They wanted a mini-summit.

Verse 2b relates Nehemiah's *perception,* surely accurate: 'they were scheming to do me harm.' Nothing very different from the thuggery in some nations today: an 'accident' occurs; a dissident strangely disappears or 'happens' to perish in a plane crash. Nehemiah has no illusions about the snakes and connivers he's dealing with. But he has his public *response* ready: 'I am doing a great work and I'm not able to come down; why should the work stop while I leave off of it and come down to you?' (v. 3). Talk is no substitute for work.

Sanballat and company were likely accurate in the intent of their scheme: if they 'took out' Nehemiah, the whole Jerusalem project would likely fizzle. However, after Nehemiah's initial retort (v. 3), they show their own helplessness or weakness in simply repeating (four times, v. 4) the same demand/request. They couldn't think of any other approach except to repeat the same ploy. The fifth time (vv. 5-7) they 'upped' the stakes. Sanballat sent an open letter. To paraphrase: 'If you don't knuckle under, Nehemiah, we'll spread rumors back at court. We'll say you're planning to revolt and that you have messianic pretensions; we'll say you are even mustering prophetic support. If you don't want this to get back to the king, you'd better play ball and meet with us.'

That is pressure that would make some pause. Nehemiah, however, simply says there is no truth in their allegations and continues on, with prayer (v. 9b). Throughout, Nehemiah seems perceptive (v. 2), tenacious (v. 4), and clear-headed (v. 8)—and yet he is weak. Otherwise, why pray this way? His prayer is simply, 'And now, strengthen my hands.'[2] There is no explicit address to God (ESV, for example, adds that). It is typical of Nehemiah's bullet petitions. It was his instinctive reaction in the midst of that turmoil. And the prayer fits perfectly. Nehemiah had just mentioned that the enemies

---

2. I am aware that Williamson (p. 249) rejects this as a petition and follows the ancient versions that take the Hebrew imperative as a first-person verb, 'I have strengthened.' The versions, however, were likely baffled by the abruptness of the Hebrew text (cf. Keil).

were thinking that with the pressure tactic the Jews' *'hands will let go of the work'*—hence Nehemiah's retort to the Lord, 'And now strengthen my *hands'* (my emphasis). Here in the thick of it all he casts himself upon God's strength.

The second threat to Nehemiah is that of **disgrace—via 'revelation'** (vv. 10-14). Shemaiah apparently wanted an interview (v. 10a), so Nehemiah calls on him.[3] Shemaiah's important visitor would be noticed and his visit might be taken as a seeking of guidance or a sign of uncertainty.[4] Shemaiah's was a counsel of panic: he wanted to take Nehemiah into 'the house of God, to the midst of the temple,' and shut up the doors because 'they' were coming to kill Nehemiah (v. 10).

The first part of Nehemiah's answer in verse 11 seems to mean 'I have more guts than that!' The second part of his answer seems to mean, 'Anyway, it's wrong.' When he asks if one 'such as I,' i.e., a layman and not a priest, can go into the temple, the expected answer is 'No.' (He was referring to the temple itself not merely its courtyards.) This was a privilege and right off limits to laymen (cf. Numbers 18:1-7, and the episode in 2 Chronicles 26:16-20).

Shemaiah's intent was to get Nehemiah to commit a ritual transgression and to thereby be discredited. But Nehemiah discerned (see v. 12) that God had not sent Shemaiah but that Tobiah and Sanballat had paid him off. When, even as a prophet, he advises something contrary to the given word of God, he is a sham. It was all a plot to lead Nehemiah into fear, into sin, and into a ruined reputation (v. 13). And Shemaiah was only part of the problem; the prophetess Noadiah and other prophets were conspiring together (v. 14), seeking to magnify Nehemiah's danger and send him into a paranoia of fear. Can you perhaps imagine Noadiah in her seductively throaty tones appealing, 'But Nehemiah, this isn't just Shemaiah's advice; *all* of us prophet-types are in agreement; this is *the Lord's* word for you.' A revelation-claim can be so convincing. They come to Nehemiah with the pitch, 'The Lord said to us ....'

---

3. Shemaiah's being 'shut up' or 'confined' could have been a 'prophetic action' reinforcing his word that Nehemiah himself needed 'seclusion' in the temple.

4. cf. Derek Kidner, *Ezra and Nehemiah*, TOTC (Leicester: Inter-Varsity, 1979), 99.

Verse 14 is a prayer for vengeance, a plea for God to 'remember' and deal with the dastardly deeds and designs of the likes of Shemaiah and his ilk. There is nothing wrong with such a prayer. What can be quite so wicked as placing one's office as bearer of God's Word up for hire, using the (alleged) Lord's Word as a tool to manipulate people and gain power over them? Even a pastor can sometimes do this by using the pulpit to spew out his venom on people who irk him and yet do it so piously under the guise of simply proclaiming 'the whole counsel of God.'

This sort of situation then highlights the *discernment* God's servants need. This kind of ploy is so tricky because it involves a revelation-claim, an alleged Word from the Lord that flaunts an aura of divine authority. Think of the Roman Catholic dogma of the immaculate conception of the Virgin Mary (i.e., that Mary was conceived without original sin). Now imagine we were living in the 1300s. Here is Bridget of Sweden who had a marvelous vision that revealed to her that the immaculate conception was true. And yet in roughly contemporary time the mystic Catherine of Siena has a wonderful vision that revealed to her that the immaculate conception was false. Two 'visions,' two revelation-claims. Who got it right? In 1854 the Roman Catholic Church voted for Bridget – and we may be pardoned for thinking it chose ill.[5] But this matter of genuineness is crucial. Leon Morris once alluded to a notice that supposedly hung in one of the museums devoted to memorabilia of the Wild West, a notice that read: 'We do not have the gun that killed Billy the Kid. Two other museums have it.'[6] So God's servants must be careful. It seems that Nehemiah could readily see through the chicanery behind Shemaiah's 'concern' (v. 12b). But we are still faced in our own day among our churches (or Christian circles) with teachers who claim they have had 'a word from the Lord,' and it is little more than self-motivated rubbish.

The third peril Nehemiah faces comes in verses 15-19, the peril of **compromise – via 'connections.'** I will try to explain

---

5. See N. R. Needham, *2000 Years of Christ's Power*, 5 vols. (London: Grace Publications, 2000), 2:275.

6. In his *Expository Reflections on the Gospel of John* (Grand Rapids: Baker, 1990), 379.

this in the process of the following discussion. These verses break down into two brief sections: an immediate summary (vv. 15-16) and an ongoing scenario (vv. 17-19). I'll focus on the latter but will first touch briefly on the former.

The wall was completed on the 25th of Elul, which would be 27 October 445 B.C.[7] In verse 16 we find an interesting reverse of the 'fearing' terminology, at least in the standard Hebrew text: 'All the nations who were around us feared.' As Fensham says:

> [I]n this chapter the idea of frightening plays an important role. In vv. 9, 13, and 14 it is said that the enemies wanted to frighten Nehemiah. But now in v. 16 the climax is reached. Nehemiah is not frightened, but the neighboring nations are. The prayer of 4:4 is fulfilled: their scorn is turned down on their own heads.[8]

Their arrogance sprang a leak (lit., 'they fell immensely in their own eyes') and they realized there must have been something 'supernatural' about the whole effort. The wall did not solve all problems, but the surrounding peoples must have sensed that it meant Judah could no longer be walked over as if it were merely a geographical marshmallow.

Now to verses 17-19. Verse 17 begins with a 'What's more' (Heb., *gam*), and then gives a time indicator – 'in those days.' That is, in the days when the wall was completed and beyond. These verses mean to depict what was going on over a period of time – an ongoing scenario. And what was that? Well, during this time Tobiah had steady back-and-forth correspondence with the more powerful folks among the Jews (v. 17). Likely, some of the 'important' citizens of Jerusalem were against (what they thought was) the isolation of Judah, perhaps for commercial reasons. Tobiah had all kinds of connections with the Jews. Many of them were 'lords of oath to him' (v. 18a) – perhaps this alludes to trading agreements they had with Tobiah and his cronies. Tobiah also had marriage ties with Jerusalem families (v. 18b); he himself had married the

---

7. Yamauchi, EBC, 4:506.

8. F. C. Fensham, *The Books of Ezra and Nehemiah,* NICOT (Grand Rapids: Eerdmans, 1982), 207.

daughter of Shecaniah, and Jehohanan his son had married the daughter of Meshullam, one of the wall repairers (3:4, 30).

That is background. Verse 19 fleshes out the muddle all this brought about. Tobiah kept sending intimidating communiques to Nehemiah, and then there was a constant stream of gossip. The pro-Tobiads kept telling Nehemiah of Tobiah's virtues and they reported everything Nehemiah had said to Tobiah. The Hebrew participles indicate this was constantly going on. So the wall was finished, but Nehemiah had to face this ongoing mess in spite of the building success. There was then a kind of '5th column' within the city, trying to wear down Nehemiah to the 'reasonable' solution of 'reconciliation' and compromise.

Here was the pestilent trouble. Tobiah had his hooks into a number of Jerusalem families and these kept up continual pressure for a 'kinder, gentler' policy toward surrounding syncretists or pagans.

Such wearing pressure is as dangerous as an overt attack, if not more so. It's the method of Mrs Potiphar who 'spoke to Joseph *day after day*' (Gen. 39:10, emphasis mine) to get him into her bed. Even devious kids know the power of such constant pressure. My mother was, I think, far too restrictive when I was a child. She was always suspicious. I had four older brothers, and if she hadn't trusted them, why should she trust me? If I asked her if I might walk 'up the lane' that went past our house, she might well refuse. The lane went, after a mile or more, to the town dump. I didn't plan to go that far. But the answer was no. But I discovered that if I intermittently kept asking that I could get her to the point of exasperation, and that fifth or sixth time would produce an unwilling, 'Oh, all right, but be back in half an hour!' It was the wearing effect of the pressure I so astutely applied that did the trick. That's the stuff Nehemiah had to face – these 'connections' Tobiah had, constantly pushing Nehemiah toward compromise. Most Christians who have their wits about them know what it is like.

We might sum up the witness of Nehemiah 6 this way:

1. God gives strength in what would alarm us (vv. 1-9)
2. God gives clarity in what would deceive us (vv. 10-14)
3. God gives tenacity in what would exhaust us (vv. 15-19)

17

Is a Reformation Beginning?
(Nehemiah 7)

If you lived in Buffalo, New York, you might have a problem. The winters, I mean. You might get hit with one of those 'lake effect' snowstorms, and dig out from it, only to get hit by another equally bad or worse snow in merely several days. You might feel this way when, as a reader, you start into Nehemiah 7. Why, we just waded through all these names and statistics in Ezra 2 – and now we get them again! Why does the Bible do this to us? Let's walk into the text; we'll look a little at the bits and pieces but primarily at the larger picture. Two main points should be made.

First, in verses 1-5 we find **some very realistic provisions**. One of these appears in the description of the circumstances in verse 1. Along with the wall being built, the doors of the gates put in place, 'the gatekeepers and singers and Levites had been appointed.' Some can't conceive that cult personnel like singers and Levites would be connected with guard duty. But given the precarious state of affairs and the sparse urban population (see v. 4), these arrangements were probably emergency measures for the meantime, a sort of co-opting additional help from the temple reserves.[1]

Nehemiah also took care to appoint qualified leadership (v. 2). Who better than his brother Hanani? He appointed him

---

1. See, e.g., H. G. M. Williamson, *Ezra, Nehemiah*, WBC (Waco: Word, 1985), 269-70. Keil likewise.

'captain of the fortress' and, lest anyone think Nehemiah was setting his brother 'in the gravy,' he noted the basis of his appointment: he was 'a faithful man' and 'fearing God more than many (others).'[2]

Then Nehemiah (or perhaps Hanani) gave additional instruction about security: 'The gates of Jerusalem are not to be opened until the heat of the day, and before you leave your posts let the doors be closed and barred' (v. 3a, NJPS). The text is a bit difficult, but on this reading the gates were to be opened later than normal and, of course, shut when guards went off duty. They would be open for a more restricted time than usual.[3] In addition, even among the residents of Jerusalem (few as they might be) guards were to be assigned to 'watch-posts,' some of them opposite their own homes (v. 3b). One would hope that this state of hyper-alert could be relaxed at some point but that was not possible in 'the present distress' (cf. 1 Cor. 7:26). Interim provisions had to be in place.

There was another problem: a lot of space in Jerusalem (relatively speaking) and few people (v. 4). Hard for a place to prosper and hard to defend it without an adequate population. Perhaps when the city was 'wall-less,' any number of the people left it for towns elsewhere in Judah. This problem won't be solved till Nehemiah 11. But here was a beginning. Nehemiah had a divine 'nudge' ('My God put it in my heart,' v. 5a) to hold an assembly in order to register people by families. This 'nudge' may have come when Nehemiah had happened on to a 'genealogical document' of those who some ninety years before had 'come up' to Jerusalem and Judah (v. 5b). He drops the matter there for the present. The document would at the very least give him an idea of the families who had probably settled in Jerusalem in the 530s B.C. (cf. vv. 7b-24).

So ... the wall is finished but life in Jerusalem is still tenuous. The wall was only a first step. Provisions must be made for defense, security, and re-population. Verses 1-5 tell us of the

---

2. Some think Nehemiah appointed Hanani 'and Hananiah' to leadership – two men with similar names. I take the text as saying, 'I commanded Hanani, my brother (i.e., Hananiah) captain of the fortress.' See on this question Andrew E. Steinmann, *Ezra and Nehemiah*, CC (St. Louis: Concordia, 2010), 481-82.

3. Others take it that the gates are not to be opened 'during the heat of the sun,' i.e., during nap time in the afternoon when guards would not be so alert.

immediate *interim* measures taken to address some of these dilemmas. Hopefully, Nehemiah and others could get beyond this 'in-between' situation. But right now certain measures had to be taken to plug the gaps in this 'meanwhile' period.

We understand interim provisions. Many of our automobiles do not have a full-size spare tire (tyre). That, manufacturers must assume, takes up too much space. So for a spare they provide a somewhat smaller tire, not so wide as a 'normal' one. Some of us call them 'do-nuts.' But they work within reason. If you have a flat, you can put your do-nut spare on and, driving carefully, get to a tire shop or garage where you can have your flat repaired or replaced. There are always some who don't understand this 'interim' provision – you see them driving down the motorway at sixty-five miles an hour on a 'do-nut.' Or, if you prefer a historical example, you might think of Dunkirk with its motley armada crossing the channel from Britain to evacuate over 338,000 British, French, and Belgian soldiers – who could live to fight again.[4] It wasn't a victory but an evacuation, but one shudders to think whether there would have been an ultimate victory without that 'in between' provision.

Stop a moment and recall that this matter of interim provisions pops up in the lives of believers constantly. You are transferred to a new community; there is no church of your preferred denomination there. There is a church, however, where the Scriptures are helpfully preached. You may, let's say, differ with that church in your view on baptism, but you fellowship there for the present period of time. Or perhaps you have children who go off to school but, for various reasons, you are convinced you should teach one child at home for a year; it may not be a practice you continue, but because of his/her special need at this point you think it wise as a temporary recourse. Or, perhaps there has been a divorce. The husband and father has walked out on his family. The (former) wife and mother might like to move, possibly for her children to be closer to grandparents. But at present she decides against it, because she doesn't want to add more upheaval to her

---

4. cf. Andrew Roberts, *Churchill: Walking with Destiny* (New York: Viking, 2018), 548-50.

children's lives at the moment; they need to be surrounded by the same church family and the stability of the same home, such as it is. Later, perhaps a change, but not for the interim. I am only trying to indicate that the principle operating in Nehemiah's challenges is one that spills over for believers at various times as well.

Secondly, note that we can trace **a very revealing pattern** between 7:6-73a (and following) and its companion list and context in Ezra 2. These two lists (Ezra 2/Nehemiah 7) of the returnees from exile sometimes diverge from each other, especially in numerical tallies. I spared readers details about all this in treating Ezra 2 – and still will try not to crush you under massive detail or endless discussion. Hopefully the following chart will provide a helpful summary and overview.

Listing / tallies in Nehemiah 7		Differences from Ezra 2
Sons of Parosh	2,172	
Shephatiah	372	
Arah	652	123 less
Pahath-moab	2,818	6 more
Elam	1,254	
Zattu	845	100 less
Zaccai	760	
Binnui	648	6 more
Bebai	628	5 more
Azgad	2,322	1,100 more
Adonikam	667	1 more
Bigvai	2,067	11 more
Adin	655	201 more
Ater	98	
Hashum	328	105 more
Bezai	324	1 more
Hariph	112	(Jorah in Ezra 2)
Gibeon	95	(Gibbar in Ezra 2)
Men of Bethlehem/		
Netophah	188	9 more
Anathoth	128	
Beth-azmaveth	42	
Kiriath-jearim etc.	743	

Listing / tallies in Nehemiah 7		Differences from Ezra 2
Ramah/Geba	621	
Michmas	122	
Bethel/Ai	123	100 less
Other Nebo	52	
[Magbish, Ezra 2 only]	156	
Other Elam	1,254	
Harim	320	
Jericho	345	
Lod, etc.	721	4 less
Senaah	3,930	300 more

Additional tallies are the same, except Nehemiah 7 has twenty more Asaph singers (v. 44), one less gatekeeper (v. 45), ten less of unproved-descent folks (v. 62), and forty-five more of male/female singers (v. 67). A total of nineteen numerical differences.

If one prefers more complication, there is also a parallel list in the apocryphal book of 1 Esdras (5:7-43). All three lists – Ezra 2, Nehemiah 7, and 1 Esdras 5 – have the same grand total of 42,360. That was a constant. But, as Derek Kidner points out, adding up the individual items in each list gives differing totals: 29,818 for Ezra, 31,089 for Nehemiah, 30,143 for 1 Esdras. At this point I think one has to be content with Kidner's conclusions:

> A comparison of the two lists reveals a startling contrast between the transmission of names and that of numbers – for the names in the two lists show only the slightest variations whereas half the numbers disagree, and do so apparently at random. The fact that the two kinds of material in the one document have fared so differently lends the weight of virtually a controlled experiment to the many other indications in the Old Testament that numbers were the bane of copyists.
>
> There is general agreement that the divergences are copying errors, arising from the special difficulty of understanding or reproducing numerical lists.[5]

---

5. Derek Kidner, *Ezra and Nehemiah*, TOTC (Leicester: Inter-Varsity, 1979), 38, 43. For what it's worth, I agree with Steinmann (pp. 165-67) that neither Ezra 2 nor Nehemiah 7 was dependent on the other but that both drew from an original document.

However, the numerical conundrums should not obscure what seems to be a very deliberate parallel between Ezra 2 (and into Ezra 3) and Nehemiah 7 (and into Nehemiah 8). The following chart traces this parallel structure:

Ezra	Nehemiah
(538 B.C. group)	(445 B.C. group)
Genealogical record, ch. 2	Genealogical impulse and record, 7:5ff.
List ends in Ezra 2:70: 'And all Israel in their towns'	List ends in Nehemiah 7:73a: 'And all Israel in their towns'
7th month and the sons of Israel in (their) towns, 3:1	7th month and the sons of Israel in their towns, 7:73b
Assembly, 3:1b People were gathered as one man to Jerusalem	Assembly, 8:1 All the people were gathered as one man to the plaza
Inauguration: Altar in the ruins, 3:3, 6 (1st day of 7th month)	Fulfillment: Law in the city, 8:1-2 (1st day of 7th month)
Feast of Tabernacles, 3:4	Feast of Tabernacles, 8:14ff.

Note how, after the genealogical listing, the text of Nehemiah echoes the same language as the Ezra text (e.g., the lingo of Nehemiah 8:1 'picks up' that of Ezra 3:1). The whole overall pattern in Nehemiah follows the exact sequence of the Ezra 2–3 passage. But the 'gathering' Nehemiah 8 describes is a wholly different 'gathering' than that of Ezra 3:1. It occurs in the same month (seventh month), yet some ninety years later. But the parallel pattern implies that the editor/author of Nehemiah wants us to view the two assemblies in tandem. He wants to draw a distinct parallel between the watershed beginning of Ezra 3 (when the returned exiles built the altar) and the 'contemporary' gathering in post-wall time after the temple had been rebuilt and the city restored. In this way the writer emphasizes that the occasion of Nehemiah 8–10 was as central and seminal as its earlier counterpart, the initial restoration under Zerubbabel. That (Ezra 2–3) had been the critical commencement, and now Nehemiah 7–8ff. is a kind of consummation. Thus the covenant renewal of Nehemiah 8–10 can be seen as placed on a plane with the altar restoration of Ezra 3. Ezra 3 stresses the people and worship, while Nehemiah 8 stresses the people and torah – one pictures worship restored, the other depicts the word restored. But this structural pattern begins in the Ezra 2 and Nehemiah 7 accounts.[6]

Isn't all this merely a bunch of literary palaver? No, it actually tells us something notable about the people of God. The Ezra 2–3 context shows they are *worship-focused*, while Nehemiah 7–8 shows they are *word-centered*. The heart of that worship begins with the restored *altar* (Ezra 3:3), the place of sacrifice where atonement takes place, while the focus of the other is on a document, 'the *book* of the law,' that instructs to faith and obedience (Neh. 8:1-2). This dual characterization is not frozen up in the fifth century BC but marks the Lord's people in our own day. It all begins with an altar, and I 'have' an altar (Heb. 13:10), where something was done for my guilt; and I have a 'book,' a Word that has been given to reveal my God and direct my way. Which means that, above all, Christians are simply and always cross-and-Bible people.[7]

---

6. My stress on this structural parallel brings to mind one of Gary Larson's 'Far Side' cartoons. Out in the old west a teamster is driving his covered wagon across the desert. He's looking straight ahead. The two oxen pulling his wagon are not. They are looking over to the right where they see the skeleton of the head of an ox sunk in the sand. The oxen are obviously pondering that they could suffer a similar ox-fate in said desert. The moral obviously is: you do well to pay attention to parallels.

7. To pick up the question in the chapter title – Is a reformation beginning? .... Well, maybe; we'll have to wait and see.

18

The Foundation of Reformation (Scripture)
(Nehemiah 8)

You are probably accustomed to a seven-day week. But in the wake of the French Revolution there were some who didn't care for a seven-day week. So they changed it: each month would be divided into three periods of ten days each. Presto: a ten-day week. Biblical scholars sometimes operate that way. Some of them don't like Nehemiah 8 being where Nehemiah 8 is. You see, if Ezra came in 458 B.C. to impose the torah in Judah (see Ezra 7), do you think he would wait around for thirteen years before he had this 'Torah Conference' in Nehemiah's time (445 B.C.)? So some critics claim Nehemiah 8 'fits' better between Ezra 8 and 9, and we can assume Ezra did his torah gig then, and went off the scene before Nehemiah arrived. Naturally, some naïve Bible reader is going to say that according to Nehemiah 8:9 both Nehemiah and Ezra were on the scene together. But the critic will smile patronizingly and say that the mention of 'Nehemiah' in 8:9 was 'probably secondary' (not original).[1] So one can run into statements like: 'Outside of Neh. 8:9 and 12:26, 36, there is no reason to think these two leaders were contemporaries.' What's so amusing (in a sad way) about that statement is that it amounts to saying: There is no reason to believe Ezra and Nehemiah were contemporaries except that the text says so.

---

1. But there is no problem in the Hebrew text of 8:9. For the confusion in the Greek versions, see Andrew E. Steinmann, *Ezra and Nehemiah,* CC (St. Louis: Concordia, 2010), 505.

Some critics worry that if we follow the text as we have it, then we know nothing of Ezra after Ezra 10 until thirteen years later in Nehemiah 8, i.e., we have no idea then what Ezra was doing in that period. There's a one-word question in answer to that: So? If Ezra–Nehemiah as we have it doesn't tell us what Ezra was doing those thirteen years, that doesn't mean he was doing nothing. It just means that the text doesn't tell us about it. Which is why I can't buy into these reconstructions: they forget we are dealing with a *selective* document. Ezra–Nehemiah gives us clips from various periods but does not even try to provide a complete or seamless historical report. With a selective document you don't expect full details or all 'gaps' to be filled in, or all head-scratchers to be answered. Many critics conveniently forget that. In Ezra–Nehemiah we are looking at significant occasions, not receiving exhaustive reporting. Nehemiah 8 is like a seven-day week – it's fine just as it is.

The focus of this chapter is the torah (instruction, teaching, 'law') of Yahweh. The word occurs nine times in the chapter. I will break down the testimony of the chapter around this theme.

First, we meet a picture of a people **delighting in the hearing of the word** (vv. 1-6). It is the first day of the seventh month (v. 2b), the festival of 'Trumpets' (cf. Lev. 23:23-25), which at least in part may explain the reason for the assembly. They congregate on the square in front of the Water Gate (v. 1a), which was on the east side above the Gihon Spring and may actually have been outside Nehemiah's wall.[2]

Take note of the *initiative* in this matter. 'All the people … told Ezra the scribe to bring the torah document of Moses that Yahweh had commanded Israel' (v. 1). This was not a movement from the top down but something driven by the 'lay' people.[3] Derek Thomas makes a telling observation here:

The fact that it is Ezra that the people call for in the opening verse of this chapter shows that he has gained their respect as

---

2. On this last matter, see Steinmann, 432, 509.

3. Goswell points out how popular expositions completely miss this point (*A Study Commentary on Ezra–Nehemiah* [Darlington: EP Books, 2013], 282-83).

a Bible teacher. It is quite possible that he has been quietly and faithfully doing the work of ministry all these years.[4]

The people seem to know that Ezra is the go-to guy if you want a Bible study. And how would they know that unless they had had some experience of his ministry among them? That's why the second sentence of the above quotation is likely a very accurate assumption. If Ezra 7:10 indicates Ezra's purpose, one would assume he would busy himself doing just that. But how heartening that the 'push' comes from the people.

In January 1742 there were 'mercy drops' in the parish of Cambuslang, indicating that a genuine revival might be coming. Near the end of the month Ingram More, a shoemaker, and Robert Bowman, a weaver, went from door to door with a petition. It is not about local government. It was a petition to request William M'Culloch, the parish minister, to give a weekly lecture. Ninety heads of households, more than half of the households in the parish, signed it. It would be held on Thursdays.[5] People wanted more of the Word – and they themselves went after it. Music to a pastor's ears.

If the people had such a desire, then we are not surprised at the *interest* they display for the Word (vv. 2-3). The general scope of the audience indicates such interest: it consists of men, women, and all who could listen with understanding (v. 2). Unlike the foolish practice of some western churches, they didn't have their middle school, junior high, and high school youth meet off by themselves for gabbing, games, refreshments, and pizza. And the torah-reading went on for 5–6 hours (v. 3a)! They were hardly ruled by the clock. Yet the reading held their attention (v. 3b).

We in the West may find this sort of interest and attention hard to imagine. And yet it seems to come into play whenever the Holy Spirit brings one of the days of the Son of Man. For example, in August 1842 William Burns preached in the churchyard at Blair Atholl (Scotland) for five hours to 4,000

---

4. Derek W. H. Thomas, *Ezra and Nehemiah*, REC (Phillipsburg, NJ: P & R, 2016), 323.

5. Arthur Fawcett, *The Cambuslang Revival* (London: Banner of Truth, 1971), 105.

people. Most of them were men, most of them stood. Or in 1839, Robert Wilson, a Congregational minister, went repeatedly to Ancrum (in the Scottish Borders). He tells of two evenings, on both of which he preached for nearly three hours, 'and yet at the close, the greatest part seemed reluctant to separate.'[6] Sometimes, as in Nehemiah 8, there is an uncommon thirst for the Word.

Reverence also pervades this occasion. Ezra is standing on a wooden 'tower' or platform made for the occasion, with his assistants around him; when he opens the torah-scroll, all the people stand (v. 5). This is a mark of reverence for the Word that is about to be read. God's people should always hold such esteem for the Word. Whether such esteem and reverence must always take the same form as in this text may be debatable. I know of churches that are sticklers for the congregation standing for the reading of Scripture. Well, look, it's right there in Nehemiah 8! But Mary (Luke 10:38ff.) *sat* at Jesus feet and listened to his teaching. My hunch is that the standing here is *descriptive* (of what the people did here) but not necessarily *prescriptive* (that we should always do so). Those who insist that worshiping assemblies today must always follow this example should also require that such assemblies bow down and put their faces to the ground (last of verse 6) – or in the carpet or on the tile or whatever floor covering the church happens to have. Nothing particularly wrong with that – more Protestants should probably be caught kneeling in public worship! And nothing wrong with standing for the reading of the Scriptures. But to make the latter a requirement goes beyond what Scripture actually requires. Perhaps we could say that what Nehemiah 8 reports in this matter is descriptive, not prescriptive, but suggestive. Reverence is normative, but the form of reverence may be optional.

Finally, notice that *worship* is mixed in with this hearing of the word: 'Then Ezra blessed Yahweh, the great God, and all the people raised their hands and answered, "Amen! Amen!"; then they bowed down and, face to the ground, prostrated

---

6. Tom Lennie, *Land of Many Revivals* (Ross-shire: Christian Focus, 2015), 352, 381.

themselves before Yahweh' (v. 6, NJB). This posture seems to signify their submission to the authority of the Word. At any rate, here is blessing and doxology directed to Yahweh, the giver of the Word. Does this not teach us that if the study of Scripture is not to degenerate into mere data-gathering or into barren intellectualism, then it must ever be mixed with praise and doxology and thanksgiving? Have you ever noticed how the apostle tends to have a 'knee-jerk' reaction of praise in response to divine truth? Note Paul's ejaculations in Romans 1:25 and 9:5; Galatians 2:20 (he just can't keep from adding 'who loved me,' etc.), and 1 Timothy 1:17.

The next picture we see is what we might label **teaching for understanding the Word** (vv. 7-8). Right off we meet with thirteen more names – privileged fellows who get to explain the torah! They are likely Levites, but we can't be dead certain.[7] At least these thirteen are 'causing the people to understand the torah' (v. 7b). Verse 8 then tells us how this took place, at least I think it does, but there is some dispute over the details.

Verse 8 begins with, 'So they read from God's torah-document.' The 'they' may refer to Ezra and his thirteen assistants in verse 4 (distinct from the group in verse 7). Some of Ezra's helpers may have relieved Ezra at certain points. Then follows that participle (of the verb *parash*) that has sucked up a lot of ink. Some think it suggests 'translating,' so that these men took the Hebrew of the read text and cast it into Aramaic for the people. But it's doubtful that these Jews had lost their touch with Hebrew in the fifth century. Others touch on the root idea of 'making distinct' and render it adverbially, 'clearly,' referring to how the torah was read. Still others take the 'making distinct' idea in the sense of breaking down the material 'section by section.' Either of the latter two views are probably close. However, if in some

---

7. After the name Pelaiah, the text (v. 7) reads, lit., 'and the Levites.' If the 'and' is explicative (equivalent to 'that is'), then the thirteen men named are Levites; or, Steinmann (pp. 503-4) expands a bit and translates 'and [the rest of] the Levites,' noting that most of the men named in the verse are probably Levites since most of the names are borne by Levites in the following chapters of Nehemiah. F. C. Fensham recalls the similar teaching ministry of Levites under King Jehoshaphat's direction in 2 Chronicles 17:7-9 (*The Books of Ezra and Nehemiah*, NICOT [Grand Rapids: Eerdmans, 1982], 217).

doubt, just keep reading the text: 'and giving the sense [or, "insight"], so that they understood the reading' (v. 8b).

We can imagine the scenario then. Ezra, or one of his assistants, reads a section of the biblical text. Then these thirteen 'expositors' (and maybe some additional Levites) circulate among the crowd, gathering groups of hearers around them, each explaining, clarifying, and perhaps applying the section of torah just read. Then Ezra would read on and the same process would recur. Depending on the nature of the passage read, sometimes the group explanation may have been brief, sometimes more involved. The intent, in any case, is to make the Word of God clear, to highlight the insight it holds, and perhaps to make its application obvious.

What a delightful task these men had – 'giving the sense so that they understood the reading.' Yet, sadly, that is not necessarily going on in our churches. I think not just of 'liberal' but of 'evangelical' churches. The preacher may read his 'text,' pick up on an idea suggested in it, and go gallivanting off through the rest of Scripture that may touch on that topic. But he does not explain or apply the text chosen. I'm sure that after some sermons I've heard I could say to any number of hearers, 'According to the sermon, what is the meaning of that text?' And they could not tell me, not because they are dense but because *the text* was not explained. Sometimes preachers seem too eager to leave behind an Old Testament text anyway, so that they can 'get to Jesus.' Maybe they begrudge the hard work that text may require and find it easier to – as one of my college professors said – 'go off crying in the blood of Christ.' Social decorum tends to restrain me. But how often I have wanted to stand up in church and cry, 'The text! The text! Explain the text!'

Verses 9-12 depict a third picture: **balancing our response to the Word**. This assembly took place on the first day of the seventh month, according to verse 2, which was the 'Feast of Trumpets' (Lev. 23:23-25 and Num. 29:1-6). The weeping of the people (v. 9) may have been over sin exposed through the reading of the torah. The weeping and sadness of verse 9 are balanced by the joy and gladness of verse 12. In verse 12 they celebrate 'because they understood the words which had been made known to them.' So the Word that saddened them (v. 9) also gladdened them (v. 12).

It is a bit of a strange scene. The people had to be *ordered* by Nehemiah *et al.* to be joyful (vv. 9-11). The idea seems to be not that mourning and weeping are wrong but that in this moment they are inappropriate – like holding a wake at a wedding. They are to have a *social* joy, not a selfish joy, for they are to send provisions to the needier folks among them (v. 10a). Their joy is also a *holy* joy. Three times the people are told that the day is 'holy' (vv. 9, 10, 11), and they are commanded to be joyful. 'The day is holy; do not be sad' (v. 11b, NJPS). Do you see the connection or the assumption? The assumption is that holiness is *not* glumness, but that holiness and happiness can be most congenial bedfellows. Then the last line of verse 10 stresses that this is a *given* joy: 'For the joy of Yahweh is your place of safety.' That is the primary argument against present sadness. Most seem to take 'the joy of Yahweh' as the joy God's people have in him, though some take it as the joy Yahweh himself has in a people willing to hear his Word (cf., e.g., Goswell). However, I would suggest 'the joy of Yahweh' is what some might call a 'genitive of source' and that it means the joy that Yahweh *gives* his people.

You might ponder that assurance, 'the joy of Yahweh is your place of safety.' Perhaps there is the suggestion that ongoing sorrow and grief, while proper at times, can leave the people of God 'unprotected'; the text implies that God-given joy fulfills a protective function in believers' lives, keeping them, perhaps, from being swallowed up in despair.

In view of all this, we can see this joy as a *corrective* joy. There is a place for loathing and grieving over sin (Ezek. 36:31). However, there are always some among the Lord's sheep who so fixate on the disaster of their sins and sinfulness, whose major tunes are all in a minor key, and who need to be told to add the tension of gladness to their grieving! Some of them need to be told that God does not intend for them to be blubbering over their sins all the time.

The last glimpse of this assembly depicts **living under the control of the Word** (vv. 13-18). The next day the heads of households met with Ezra for ongoing Bible study (v. 13). They found written in the torah the regulations about the Feast of Tabernacles (or, Booths; see Leviticus 23:33-43, especially 40, 42-43, and Deuteronomy 16:13-15, with the emphasis on joy in the latter passage). There is a beautiful simplicity in the sequence: 'they found it written in the torah' (v. 14a) and 'so the people went out and brought in (branches) and made for themselves booths' (v. 16a). The Bible said they were to do it, so they did. Verse 16 indicates the various locations of their booths, while verse 17 emphasizes the uniqueness of the celebration.[8]

The celebration of 'Tabernacles,' with the people camping out in their makeshift lean-tos, was an appropriate word to post-exilic Judah, as it should be to the Lord's people in all ages. Tabernacles was meant to force Israel to recall their tenuous post-Egypt existence on the wilderness journey. In the midst of Israel's settled life in the land they were to remember their former hand-to-mouth existence, to recall how fragile life is. In the middle of what was also a harvest festival they remember that life *can* be a wilderness, and that whether it has been manna in the wilderness (Exod. 16) or harvest in the land, their only sustainer is Yahweh. They must never forget their humiliation in the wilderness (Deut. 8:2-3) nor the One who sustained them through it.

Nehemiah 8 tells us that if there is to be a reformation in 445 B.C., it must begin with a re-discovery of Scripture and obedience to it.

---

8. There is some question about the claim of verse 17. Just what hadn't been done since the days of Joshua the son of Nun? The simplest answer seems to be that Israel had not actually dwelt in booths since Joshua's time when they celebrated the feast. They *had* celebrated it (see Ezra 3:4, for example) but apparently had done so without actually making the lean-tos and camping out in them. For this view, see C. F. Keil, *The Books of Ezra, Nehemiah, and Esther*, Biblical Commentary on the Old Testament (reprint ed., Grand Rapids: Eerdmans, 1966), 234.

19

The Preparation for Reformation (Prayer)
(Nehemiah 9)

This chapter flows properly on from the previous one. It contains a lengthy prayer and will take us a bit to take it all in. It is probably too much to call this praying a 'condition' for reformation (that would go beyond the text), but surely it may be viewed as a *preparation* for reformation.

I want to consider the prelude to the prayer (vv. 1-5) before looking at the prayer itself in more detail. Verse 1 tells of the people's *decision* and makes it clear that they are now determined to get back to the business of 8:9 that had had them so upset. They gather on the 24th of the seventh month, two days after their celebration of the Feast of Tabernacles (last of chapter 8). Those who stayed on for this 'were doing so by deliberate choice.'[1]

Their *agenda* is clear: 'they stood and confessed their sins and the iniquities of their fathers' (v. 2). Note the sheer scope of that; it's obviously going to take some time to do that, which suggests we should think of the *time* it takes to confess well. There can be no short cuts here. And their *procedure* seems to be a carryover from chapter 8. Apparently, they read from the torah-book for about three hours, then for another three hours confess sins and

---

1. Derek Kidner, *Ezra and Nehemiah*, TOTC (Leicester: Inter-Varsity, 1979), 110.

worship (v. 3). It is the Word of God that incites and informs confession and worship.[2]

Finally, notice their *leaders* on this occasion, who seem to be Levites. Those mentioned in verse 5 are not exactly the same as those mentioned in verse 4, but why should that be a big problem? I would take the words uttered in verse 5b as both a call to prayer and an introduction to prayer. RSV and NRSV insert 'And Ezra said' at the beginning of verse 6 (following LXX), but it's not in the Hebrew text; the words of the following prayer come from the Levites. They begin with a call to worship: 'Stand up and bless Yahweh your God (who is) from everlasting to everlasting!' (v. 5b). Once more, Kidner nicely catches the irony of the moment: 'the barely habitable city, the encircling heathen, and the poverty and seeming insignificance of the Jews are all transcended by the glorious reality of God.'[3]

Now let us consider the prayer itself, which covers the whole range of historical moments – creation (v. 6), Abraham (vv. 7-8), the exodus (vv. 9-12), Sinai (vv. 13-14), the wilderness (vv. 15ff.), the conquest (vv. 22-25), the judges and following (vv. 26ff.). We can trace the prayer in three major segments (vv. 6-15, 16-31, 32-37).

First, then, the Levites' prayer speaks to Yahweh of **the gifts of his grace** (vv. 6-15). The majority of this section focuses on Yahweh as redeemer. However, verse 6 expresses homage to Yahweh as *creator*. Both verses 6 and 7 begin with the same phrase (lit., 'You [are] he'), implying that the creator of verse 6 and the redeemer of verse 7 are one and the same. Verse 6 lauds Yahweh as not only creator of all things (heaven, earth, seas and their contents; note four uses of 'all') but as life-giver and sustainer as well – 'you keep giving life to all of them.'[4] What he makes he sustains; what he brings into being he preserves – an important principle to remember. And for all this he receives worship

---

2. 'In light of the previous chapter we may take it that the reading was no mere stream of words, but punctuated with explanatory comments and applications to the present situation' (Kidner, 110).

3. Kidner, 111.

4. The Hebrew participle indicates continuous action.

from those conscious, invisible (to us) beings called the 'heavenly hosts.'

Verse 6 performs a valuable theological role in this prayer. Note that the Bible never allows you to bifurcate Yahweh as creator or redeemer. The Bible will not allow you to play creation over against redemption or vice versa. If you ignore redemption, you lose the cross; if you ignore creation, you lose the world.

I think the best way to get at 'the gifts of his grace' here is to highlight the kind of God who is at work. And right off we are told that this massive, creating, preserving God of verse 6 is also *the calling God* of verse 7: 'who chose Abram and brought him out of Ur of the Chaldees and designated his name Abraham.' After the immense reaches of verse 6, the particular name of verse 7 is a bit staggering. Quite a stretch from a vast creation and innumerable 'hosts' to a single Mesopotamian idolater (see Josh. 24:2) who is called by name. One can't reproduce the wonder but can yet see the principle in the ethos of the Truman White House. Harry and Bess Truman did not act like aristocrats (as did some presidential couples before and after them). Truman insisted on calling kitchen staff by first name. His driver was a Secret Service member by name of Floyd Boring. In the first conversation Truman had with him, he asked him what his role was and was told that he (Boring) was assigned as Truman's driver. Truman's questions followed: 'Well, could you tell me your name?' Being told, he asked, 'You don't mind if I call you Floyd, do you?'[5] Likewise, Abram. God chose and called Abram by name. And some of us have never recovered from the wonder of it (John 10:3).

Yahweh is also *the promising God* (v. 8). The promise was to give Abraham's seed the land of the Canaanites and those other '-ites.' But that promise was wrapped up in a covenant Yahweh 'cut' with Abraham (see Gen. 15:7-21). The promise is the heart of the covenant, but the covenant is the 'wrapper' God puts around the promise to make us more sure of the promise. The text summarizes covenant: (1) the root of covenant is election, going back to verse 7, 'who chose Abram';

---

5. A. J. Baime, *The Accidental President* (Boston: Mariner Books. 2018), 198.

(2) the concern of covenant is place (verse 8b, the land); it's as if Yahweh says to Israel, 'I go to prepare a place for you'; and (3) the anchor of covenant is fidelity (verse 8d), 'And you have made good your promises' (NJB). For Israel the promising God is the reliable God, something pagans had no conception of. Yahweh makes and keeps promises but no pagan could expect that of his/her deity. In the 'Gilgamesh Epic' the goddess Ishtar offers herself in marriage to Gilgamesh with lavish promises, but Gilgamesh rejects her 'proposal' in the most scathing terms, citing her past pattern of infidelities.[6] Not so Yahweh – a faithful God is himself a gift of grace.

Next, the prayer remembers Yahweh as *the delivering God* (vv. 9-11). The note of compassion is not missing here, for Yahweh saw Israel's affliction and heard their cry (v. 9), but verses 10-11 stress the judgment aspect of Yahweh's deliverance: the plagues that crinkled Egypt's arrogance and the sea that swept their troops into Sheol. This is the way divine deliverance works. The protection of God's people at some point involves the destruction of their enemies. Otherwise there can be no real deliverance. Luther understood this well. He exhorted his readers to pray for the salvation of their enemies but then also admitted:

> I cannot pray without cursing at the same time. If I say: 'Hallowed be Thy name,' I must thereby say: May the names of the papists and all who blaspheme Thy name be accursed, condemned, and dishonored. If I say: 'Thy kingdom come,' I must thereby say: May the papacy, together with all kingdoms on earth that are opposed to Thy kingdom, be accursed, condemned, and destroyed. If I say: 'Thy will be done,' I must thereby say: May the plans and plots of the papists and of all who strive against Thy will and counsel be accursed, condemned, dishonored, and be brought to naught.[7]

You might wish Luther was not so brutal in his prayers, at least against the Romanists of his day. Some might claim that

---

6. Alexander Heidel, *The Gilgamesh Epic and Old Testament Parallels* (Chicago: Phoenix Books, 1963), 7, 50.

7. Quoted in Brian G. Najapfour, 'Martin Luther on Prayer and Reformation,' in *Taking Hold of God*, ed. Joel R. Beeke and Brian G. Najapfour (Grand Rapids: Reformation Heritage, 2011), 25-26.

it's merely an outburst of his salty character. No, he's simply perceptive. He knows that if God's name is to be hallowed then everything that demeans that name must be eliminated. The 'Lord's Prayer' rightly understood is a terribly lethal prayer. It recognizes that only a judging God can be a delivering God.

Then the prayer celebrates Yahweh as *the providing God* (vv. 12-15). His provision is multi-faceted. He provides guidance for their journey, the pillar of cloud and of fire (v. 12). He doesn't deliver and then leave them to wander in a dither. He provides direction for living (vv. 13-14). Note the positive spin on Sinai here. It was the place where God *gave* his people good rules and laws and statutes and commandments and sabbath, so that they would know how to live as a delivered people. Seeing the Sinai revelation as this Scripture and prayer place it, i.e., in the context of redemption, shows that Law is a gift of grace for a redeemed people. Sinai is the assurance that Yahweh does not redeem a people from bondage only to abandon them to ambiguity. The Law is the *clarity* of a gracious God who refuses to leave his people in limbo about what pleases him. And then the prayer recalls Exodus 16 and 17 (v. 15), how Yahweh provides sustenance in their need. It was not 'normal' provision but provided in an unguessable way – bread 'from heaven' and water 'from a rock.' So here is a God who pursues his deliverance with all sorts of provision.

Here then (vv. 6-15) the prayer surveys these gifts of Yahweh's grace but in a way that shows Yahweh himself to be the finest 'gift'; there is a 'surpassing worth' (cf. Phil. 3:8) in having him as your God.

In the second major section of the prayer the Levites speak of **the tenacity of his goodness** (vv. 16-31). This segment breaks down into two sub-sections:

1. Rebellion – and patience and provision (vv. 16-25)
2. Rebellion – and severity and kindness (vv. 26-31)

Look first at verses 16-25. After repeated use of the second person, highlighting all that 'you' (Yahweh) had done in verses 9-15, there comes an emphatic third person, 'But they, on their part …' (v. 16a). The ancestors of the pray-ers 'acted arrogantly.' The verb (Heb., *zid*) was used also in verse 10, where it refers to the Egyptians acting arrogantly. So here

(v. 16) Israel behaves as Egyptians. There is an Egyptian nature within Israel.

Verses 16-17a use very strong language. This was no momentary lapse on Israel's part. Everything speaks of deliberate, open-eyed resistance to God's will. Rebellion expressed in five specific statements (16b-17a). Then there was the rebellion par excellence, the making and worship of the golden calf in Exodus 32. Yet this prayer toys with the incredible, confessing outrageous things like 'But you are a God of forgivenesses' (lit., note the plural; v. 17b). Twice they confess, 'You did not forsake them' (vv. 17, 19). Yahweh really is like Exodus 34:6 says he is. So, after the vicious rebellion of verses 16-18, we read of the ongoing provision of verses 19-25 – there was *still* Yahweh's continuing care in the wilderness (vv. 19-21) and in his giving them the land (vv. 22-25) in the conquest of turf both east (v. 22) and west (vv. 24-25) of the Jordan. There's a statement in verse 21 that sums up the care in the wilderness: 'Forty years you sustained them in the wilderness.' And the last of verse 25 sums up the gift of the land: 'and [they] revelled in your great goodness' (NJB). All this provision comes in the wake – and in spite of – their stubborn disobedience. Remembering this context leads to an important observation: God's gifts are no sign of our righteousness.

Verses 26-31 take us beyond the conquest and into the time of the judges. But it's the same boring song (v. 26). As in a previous generation (v. 18), Israel again commits 'great acts of contempt' (v. 26; GW renders, 'outrageous sins'). For this Yahweh brings them into distress (v. 27a), but the wonder is that there is distress *and* deliverance (v. 27b). But nothing changes. The yo-yo pattern bounces between misery and mercy (v. 28). Verses 29-31 could almost be read as a sad summary of all 1 Kings 12–2 Kings 25. The use of the verb *zid*, 'to act arrogantly,' in verse 29 harks back to its use in verse 16, and so much as says, 'You see, nothing has changed throughout their history.' In one sense, the radical NT scholar, Rudolf Bultmann, was right: Israel's history is a history of *miscarriage*. They are a people who perpetually fail in their basic covenant fidelity.

The previous sub-point (vv. 16-25) carried the message, 'You rebelled – and God still provides.' The second sub-point (vv. 26-31) says, 'You rebelled – and you still exist.' But that is only due to Yahweh's compassions (vv. 27, 28, 31). It's as if the pray-ers are saying: You have given us up, but you have not finished us off. I suppose the tale can be told in the 'many' clauses:

> *Many times* you rescued them (28)
> You bore with them for *many years* (30)
> In your *many compassions* you did not make an end of
> 　　them (31)

Those praying this prayer are standing amazed at the inexplicable tenacity of Yahweh's goodness.

Brian Kelly has written a book called *Best Little Stories from World War II*. In it he tells of Bill Miller, who, in February 1940, had just purchased his first car. Late at night he started home from Harrisburg, Pennsylvania; three feet of snow covered the ground but the roads were clear – except they were wet and Miller didn't think about them being frozen under the night temperatures. Insanely, he thought he'd see how fast his new car would go. He remembered 110 miles an hour, before the curve, when the brakes locked, he hit a culvert, shot through the windshield and was buried in snow. A passing motorist and his friend found Miller, took him to a hospital, and after four days in a coma, Miller was told a fellow named Warren Felty had rescued him.

Five years later, Miller, a B-17 pilot who had been shot down over Germany, was one of a horde of allied POWs the Germans were herding on a seventy-five-mile march; there were two feet of snow on the ground, temperatures down to zero. All the POWs were exhausted; it was every man for himself. Miller could scarcely put one foot in front of another and at last fell out and into a snow bank; succumbing to sleep there would mean certain death. But then someone was kicking, shaking, pulling him out of the snow bank and dragging him on. It was another POW who'd been herded into the same march. In fact, it was Warren Felty, who had saved Miller's life five years before and 4,000 miles away.

With the war over, Bill Miller is back in Pennsylvania having breakfast at a roadside restaurant and about to lose his job because he could not get a local distributor for his company's products. A passing motorist who had never stopped at this restaurant decided to do so. He happened to meet Miller and within two hours made arrangements for his company to serve as Miller's needed distributor. Yes, the motorist was Warren Felty. Miller probably thought it very bizarre. It was as if he couldn't 'shake' Warren Felty. He just always showed up! I think that's the sense those praying this prayer have: for all our folly and sin we 'just can't shake' Yahweh – he just won't let go of us!

Now in the third section of the prayer, the Levites speak of **the rightness of his justice** (vv. 32-37). This section of the prayer begins with 'And now ....' The Levites and assembly are ceasing their historical review and coming to the contemporary scene. In this section they ask God to hear and look upon ...

1. *Their cry (v. 32)*

   They ask the Lord not to look on all this history of troubles (lit., hardship, weariness) as trivial. They have been ravaged by outsiders, especially from the times when the kings of Assyria held dominance (722 B.C. and following, if not before) up to the present time. There was Assyria, then Babylon, and now Persia.

2. *Their confession (vv. 33-35)*

   They confess, however, that Yahweh has acted rightly in all the distress he has brought upon them. They clearly admit the rightness of Yahweh's ways and the persisting sin of Israel.

3. *Their condition (vv. 36-37)*

   Here is their condition at the current moment. Twice they state those heart-rending words: 'We are slaves' (v. 36). They are an anomaly – they are in the land Yahweh 'gave' their fathers but are slaves in it. They may be in the land, but they are ruled and taxed by others.

The prayer of chapter 9 ends *descriptively*, as if to say, 'This is our situation.' There is no overt request, no particular petition here. Rather they are saying, 'Here is our condition.' End of prayer. But it's not so mute as it seems.

We were in Jackson, Mississippi, when our sons were young. In the church where we worshiped there was an elder, Mr McDiarmid. He was far more than an elder; he was the source of weekly treasures. All the children knew Mr McDiarmid seemed to always have an endless supply of candy or gum to parcel out after church. I vividly recall one after-church scene when our youngest, who was probably four, went up to Mr M, stood in front of him, and simply looked up to all six feet of him. He didn't say anything, just stood and gazed. But his benefactor seemed to interpret it all as a mute petition. That seems to be the state of things at the end of the prayer in Nehemiah 9. Verses 36-37 seem to carry an implied petition in light of the whole prayer. Here, at the end, Israel seems to be asking: 'Have your "great compassions" altogether ceased? Have your mercies completely dried up? You will not now "forsake" what you have refused to forsake so far …, will you?'

20

The Structure for Reformation (Covenant)
(Nehemiah 10)

Nehemiah 9 and 10 are like eating a slice of pizza. You take a bite and find that all the mozzarella cheese on that slice comes sliding off with that initial bite. It's all 'connected.' Actually, in our English Bibles chapter 10 really starts in 9:38 (which is 10:1 in the Hebrew text), so we are looking at 9:38–10:39. Chapter 9, verse 38 begins with, 'Now in view of all this.' In view of what? In view of the prayer of repentance in chapter 9. In short, here (in chapter 10) is what repentance leads to, what it looks like at this point. The first phrase of 9:38 ties all of chapter 10 tightly to chapter 9. So, they say, we are 'cutting' a firm commitment (Heb., *'amanah*) 'and putting it in writing.' Chapter 10 is that written document that depicts what their repentance will look like in practice. There is scarcely a break at all between the prayer of chapter 9 and the covenant of chapter 10. True, the prayer of chapter 9 concludes with the end of verse 37, but the first-person plurals ('we,' 'us,' 'our') of direct speech continue on (9:38; 10:30ff.) all the way to the end (10:39).[1] So then, the prayer of chapter 9 highlights Israel's ongoing history of apostasy and infidelity. What then can Judah do but repent? But

---

1. Gregory Goswell, *A Study Commentary on Ezra–Nehemiah* (Darlington: EP Books, 2013), 312.

how do you repent? Chapter 10 suggests that covenant can be the vehicle for repentance.[2]

First off, let us notice **the definiteness of the covenant** – we see this primarily in the lists of names (vv. 1-17). These names include both the leadership and the laity. Nehemiah and Zedekiah (v. 1), major officials, seem set off by themselves. Then we meet with twenty-one priests, seventeen Levites, and forty-four lay people. The priests are listed mostly according to family names (vv. 2-8),[3] followed by the Levites, listed as individuals rather than families (vv. 9-13),[4] and then the lay leaders (vv. 14-27). Some of these last seem to be names of ancestral houses and some of individuals.[5] The names of ancestors 'indicates that the entire family descended from that ancestor pledged themselves to uphold the solemn agreement.'[6]

The number of names listed probably indicates that this covenant measure enjoyed wide support. However, the list of names may well be representative rather than exhaustive. The way verses 28-29 read seems to indicate that there were other priests, Levites, and various servants who did not actually sign the document and yet entirely supported it. Moreover, we don't know if there were a number who refused to sign and/or did not agree with this measure, or how many may have belonged to such a group.[7]

But the names are significant, for a name can commit one – and get one in trouble. UK readers must forgive me mentioning the American Declaration of Independence. It

---

2. Some critics want to play 'musical chairs' with chapter 10, insisting that it fits much better after chapter 13 (e.g., D. J. A. Clines, *Ezra, Nehemiah, Esther*, NCBC [Grand Rapids: Eerdmans, 1984], 199-200, and H. G. M. Williamson, *Ezra, Nehemiah*, WBC [Waco: Word, 1985], 325-26, 330-31). However, their claims are well answered by Goswell (p. 315), and especially by Gary V. Smith, *Ezra–Nehemiah*, ZECOT (Grand Rapids: Zondervan, 2022), in footnote 2, pp. 397-98.

3. Clines worries that Ezra's name is missing (p. 199), but he is lurking behind his ancestor, Seraiah (v. 2a; cf. Ezra 7:1; see Derek Kidner, *Ezra and Nehemiah*, TOTC [Leicester: Inter-Varsity, 1979], 114).

4. A number of these have already been met in 8:7 and 9:4-5.

5. 'Fourteen of the first eighteen names in verses 14ff. occur in the list of ancestral families in Ezra 2:3-20' (Andrew E. Steinmann, *Ezra and Nehemiah*, CC [St. Louis: Concordia, 2010], 560).

6. Steinmann, 557.

7. Gary Smith (pp. 405-6) has some useful observations on these items.

was likely not fully signed until August 1776, but the fifty-six signers knew that by doing so they were committing high treason against the crown. By the end of the war, almost every one of the signers had lost his property and many had lost wives and children to British guns and prisons.[8] That American congress was skilled at bungling any number of matters, but at least those men knew what signing their names and pledging their 'lives, fortunes, and sacred honor' might cost them. Because they signed their names. There is something so definite about that. Doing so, you commit yourself, you take a stand. Was that not the case here in Nehemiah 10? Gary Smith has it right: 'Each person who printed his name (with a seal or in his handwriting) was sending a message to his family and friends that he was setting a new direction for the extended family.'[9]

Whether there is a specific document or not, doesn't this issue of 'definiteness' always hang over Christ's disciples? I like that close of the crucifixion account in John's gospel. Here is Joseph of Arimathea, who is a disciple of Jesus, 'but secretly, for fear of the Jews.' But the fear has gone. He goes to Pilate to get possession of Jesus' body. He comes and takes away the body. And now everybody knew. And there is Nicodemus beside him, lugging burial preparations (John 19:38-39). Now the Sanhedrin knows. They have taken a stand. It's as if Joseph and Nicodemus had signed their names at the foot of the cross.

Secondly, we note **the solemnity of the covenant** in verses 28-29. This covenant is taking in a wide swath of the people. There are many others in addition to the 'signers' who will enter into this covenant, and they are not limited to heads of households but include wives and children, and apparently quite young children (so long as they can understand). These (v. 28) are joining with the others (perhaps those in vv. 1-27) and are 'entering into a curse and an oath' to 'walk in the torah of God' (v. 29). This last means that they intend 'to keep and to do all the commandments of Yahweh our Lord and

---

8. Larry Schweikart and Michael Allen, *A Patriot's History of the United States* (New York: Sentinel, 2004), 81.

9. Smith, 405.

his rules and his statutes' (v. 29b). Someone may get nervous here and yammer about 'legalism.' But this is not legalism. This is simply a back-to-the-Bible movement. And there's nothing legalistic about wanting to obey what the Bible says we should do.

There is, however, something quite serious here: they are entering into 'a curse and an oath.' What does that mean? It was an oath one took when making covenant promises that if one didn't keep those commitments, God would inflict the curses of the covenant for such covenant-breaking. There's a vivid illustration of this in Jeremiah 34. One needs to read the whole chapter to pull together all the parts. It was near 587 B.C. and the Babylonians were about to crush Jerusalem. King Zedekiah and the upper crusts decided to free their Hebrew slaves – after all, what use would they be if everything was going to rack and ruin anyway? But then the Babylonians lifted the siege in order to go meet an Egyptian force that was making a token attempt to relieve Jerusalem. Then the men of Judah decided they had done a stupid thing – they could use those slaves after all. So they re-enslaved them, going back on their word. But that word had been a covenant-word. They had 'cut' a covenant over it. They had cut a calf down the middle and had walked between the two pieces. That was 'entering into the curse of the covenant.' As they walked between that double carcass, they were saying, 'If we do not keep our word in this covenant, may what happened to this calf happen to us.' Because they broke their word, Yahweh said that was precisely going to be their fate:

> And the men who transgressed my covenant and did not keep the terms of the covenant which they made before me, I will make like the calf which they cut in two and passed between its parts (Jer. 34:18, RSV).

Then he delineated how that would take place (vv. 20-22).

All that is not to say that we should not make commitments to the Lord. This 'curse and oath' in Nehemiah 10:29 is not meant to frighten us but to sober us. 'Be not rash with your mouth, nor let your heart be hasty to utter a word before God, for God is in heaven, and you upon earth; therefore, let your words be few' (Eccles. 5:2, RSV). Be very careful about claiming things like 'Even though they all fall away, I will not' (Mark 14:29).

Thirdly, the text brings us down to **the specifics of the covenant** (vv. 30-39). Covenant renewal cannot thrive on generalities and vague resolutions. Covenant is willing to itemize its commitments.

On this occasion these commitments focus on five concerns: (1) marriage (v. 30); (2) sabbath (v. 31); (3) funds for worship maintenance (vv. 32-33); (4) firewood (v. 34); and (5) offerings (vv. 35-39). Of these five concerns, the first two involve *separation* (from pagans), the latter three *support* (for worship).

Let's touch on the 'separation' items first (vv. 30-31). In line with Exodus 34:11-16 and Deuteronomy 7:1-4, the people pledge not to let their sons or daughters intermarry with pagan peoples around them (v. 30). To be sure, the specific pagan peoples may now have other names. There are no Girgashites or Perizzites or Jebusites around in 445 B.C. Obviously, the particulars have changed (there are different '-ites' now) but the principle has not: careful separation from pagans. They knew how to apply the torah to their own day. Both Exodus and Deuteronomy pulled no punches over the peril involved. Intermarry with pagans and you can kiss covenant faith goodbye. Marital amalgamation was a sure path to castrating faithful devotion to Yahweh. You may raise Baal worshipers that way but not Yahweh disciples.

Then there was the sabbath (v. 31). They would refrain from commercial haggling on the sabbath and also keep the provisions for the 'sabbatical' year (Exod. 23:10-11; Deut. 15:1-2). If pagans brought in grain and stuff to sell on the sabbath, people in Judah would not strictly be 'working' on the sabbath by buying such wares. But this covenanting people believed they could break the sabbath not only by work but by clutter. So they would boycott the pagans. The sabbath was their culture-defying tool.[10]

---

10. To gain further appreciation for the biblical sabbath, cf. Jewish scholar Nahum Sarna's *Exploring Exodus* (New York: Schocken, 1986), 145-48. For a helpful and careful discussion of the fourth commandment, see J. Douma, *The Ten Commandments* (Phillipsburg, NJ: P & R, 1996), 109-60.

By their marriage and sabbath commitments the people of Judah were refusing to let the world squeeze them into its mold (cf. J. B. Phillips' translation of Romans 12:2).

The second category of commitments centers on the support the people pledge in order to maintain worship (vv. 32-39). We run into the phrase 'the house of our God' nine times in this section (actually, eight times, once it is 'the house of Yahweh,' v. 35). They are concerned about carrying on temple worship.

The people then pledge funds for the maintenance of temple worship (vv. 32-33), to provide materials for worship and for the upkeep of the temple. Some see Exodus 30:11-16 as a kind of precedent, but there is no indication in that passage that the half-shekel 'tax' imposed there was a yearly affair – at most it was to be imposed whenever there was a census. Here the people each pledge a third of a shekel annually. Over the years there had been Persian subsidies for Jerusalem worship (Ezra 6:8-10; 7:21-23), but who knows how long that lasted; it was not wise to be dependent on such grants. But notice that more is at stake here than stones and mortar and grain and animals: this worship provides sin offerings 'to make atonement for Israel.' This is the place where sacrifices are killed and blood is spilt and sins are forgiven. This doesn't just involve a system but their life.

Then there is the firewood (v. 34). That may seem like a picky detail scarcely worth dragging into the provisions of a solemn religious agreement. But it's something that could easily fall through the cracks. Along with the continuing offering of sacrifices (Lev. 6:12-13) goes an ongoing need for fuel. Casting lots they set up a definite schedule for certain families to supply firewood for the altar. What seems pedantic is often crucial. In 1948 an Arab force was assaulting Kastel. The Jews had taken the village, but the Arabs under Kamal Irekat were driving the Jewish force back. Suddenly the Arab assault stopped. They had run out of ammunition. No one had been concerned for the ammunition supply.[11] It was merely a detail, but it seems to me it was rather important. So

11. Larry Collins and Dominique LaPierre, *O Jerusalem!* (New York: Simon and Schuster, 1972), 266-67.

here. No wood, no worship. Minor matters can be essential matters. There is a principle here that Christian believers can exploit to their profit.

Finally, the people pledge to bring the requisite offerings to the temple (vv. 35-39). These provisions deal with the sustaining of the temple worship itself, particularly the temple staff (priests, Levites; see, more fully, Numbers 18:8-32). The first-born of their sons and livestock (presumably of unclean animals) could be redeemed by a payment (Num. 18:15-16); but first-born of clean animals (herds and flocks) are brought.[12] Along with these they will bring the prescribed offerings of produce for the Levites and the priests; a priest will oversee the Levites' work in collecting the specified tithes; and the Levites will be careful to tithe what they themselves receive for the priests (vv. 37-39). Such provisions are for those who serve in the temple. Verse 39b sums up the intent behind verses 32-39: 'We will not neglect the house of our God.'

This giving to support temple personnel was crucial in order to maintain the temple worship. Otherwise, as happened later (13:10), Levites and others had to drop temple duty in order to scrounge out a living for themselves. Those who serve in the temple should live by the temple (cf. 1 Cor. 9:13-14). A similar obligation rests on Christian congregations to support adequately those who preach to and pastor them. I have copies of my father's annual pastor's reports to the congregations he served. My father was cut from a different bolt of cloth and did not mind being direct with his people. So I have his 'annual report' for 1932. Granted, it was the 'Depression' era, but he also had at that time a wife and three sons – and three congregations to serve. At the end of the report he said that the salary from Sandy Lake was $250 behind, which, added to the $100 arrears from the year before, meant that church was $350 in arrears. The North Sandy salary was $138.44 behind in the current year and was $110.70 behind the year before, which meant that church was $249.14 in arrears. He put it right out there in his annual report! Who's to say he was 'wrong'? They had pledged something to him and he was holding them to it. Many churches today don't need to be reminded

---

12. Goswell, 320.

of the principle behind Nehemiah 10:35-39; they generously and adequately support their pastors and teachers. And yet there are still miserly congregations out there whose budget committees should be given shock treatments to rouse them to pay a living wage to those serving them.

Some of these items in the covenant may not especially grab our interest, and so we may be prone to dismiss them. But the basic matters in this covenant are still 'live' issues for Christians, namely, marriage, sabbath (largely ignored though it is), and giving. Don't, however, look on the covenant as a piece of legalism, as merely a document with an eye for picky detail. Rather, what we have in Nehemiah 10 are 'fruits that show repentance' (Luke 3:8). Some of John the Baptist's audience in Luke 3 asked him what those 'fruits' might be that show genuine repentance, and he specified generosity (v. 11), honesty (v. 13), and contentment (v. 14). That is the sort of thing happening in Nehemiah 10: here is brokenness of heart (remember Neh. 9) that is not content to moan and groan, but to use paper and ink and to itemize precisely how it will repent.

21

The Order of the People of the Lord
(Nehemiah 11:1–12:26)

By now, in Ezra–Nehemiah you have noticed how the Bible loves lists. Especially lists of people. And this section of Nehemiah seems to be nothing but lists. Western readers may be aggravated at this, but the Bible is more patient – it seems to think names matter and that people are significant. Moreover, Bible lists often 'tell' us things. Here in Nehemiah 11:1–12:26 they show us how God's people ordered their lives during the tenure of Nehemiah. We can trace this theme under three heads.

The first head can be called **anchoring the city** (11:1-24). Here we must remember the dilemma of 7:4: 'The city was stretched out and large, while the people in it were few and not enough houses were built' (Fensham). So here verses 1-2 tell of *the plan to be followed*. It appears that the leaders already lived in Jerusalem – but how to bulk up the general population?

The need was acute. It may be 'the holy city' (vv. 1, 18) but in its present situation it was a far cry from having all nations streaming to it as depicted in Isaiah 2. As a house deteriorates when no one lives in it, so Jerusalem will remain vulnerable without sufficient population. Having a refurbished wall is essential, but with few living behind the wall, it becomes a half-solution. Currently, there were not enough Jews living in it to make it secure. The holy city is a bleak city.

The people, however, had recourse to a solution: they would tithe people![1] One in ten living in the territory of Judah would be drafted to relocate and reside in Jerusalem (v. 1b). How to do this? By casting lots. That way none of those selected could blame certain leaders, or Nehemiah, for their selection. Rather, since it was by lot, they had been drafted by the Lord (see Proverbs 16:33)! They accepted it as a sovereign direction. They 'willingly settled in Jerusalem' (v. 2, NJPS).

This re-settlement would, probably, in most cases, involve sacrifice. Because they did this willingly does not mean they did it thrillingly. Why would these people be commended unless they did what was *inconvenient* for them? They did not prefer to live in Jerusalem or they would have already been settled there. They face, then, the trouble of uprooting themselves from homes, leaving them for the city. Would it involve in some cases a change of work, of means of livelihood? In any case, a sacrifice was made for the people of God. A question then faces us: Is this ever a move we are called to make? Are there times where self-denial must take precedence over preferences, and when consideration for the people of God must be placed above my interests?

So much for the plan. The text goes on to specify *the people who are settled* (vv. 3-24).[2] The pattern is:

Those from Judah, vv. 4-6
Those from Benjamin, vv. 7-9
Priests, vv. 10-14
Levites, vv. 15-18
Gatekeepers, v. 19
Additional notes / arrangements, vv. 20-24

---

1. Goswell points out that this decision is *not* attributed to Nehemiah (*A Study Commentary on Ezra–Nehemiah* [Darlington: EP Books, 2013], 324). Expositors who fixate on touting Nehemiah as a model of leadership can fail to note such items.

2. First Chronicles 9 has a somewhat parallel list but it's difficult to figure out the relation between the two. Jacob Myers claims that the traditional Hebrew text has about 81 names for Nehemiah 11 and about 71 for Chronicles, of which only about 35 are the same or nearly so (*1 Chronicles*, AB [Garden City, NY: Doubleday, 1965], 67). cf. Martin J. Selman, *1 Chronicles*, TOTC (Leicester: Inter-Varsity, 1994), 123-24, who suggests the Chronicles account is a bit later than that in Nehemiah.

Most of the primary names seem to refer to the heads of groups and these 'primaries' are followed by a barrage of names tracing their descent. For Judah, for example, the prime names are Athaiah (v. 4) and Maaseiah (v. 5), with the former given a six-step pedigree and the latter a seven-step one. The same pattern with Sallu in verse 7, Seraiah in verse 11, Adaiah in verse 12, and so on. If we follow the tallies given for the various groups (vv. 6, 8, 12, 13, 14, 18, 19; and none of the numbers are round numbers) we come up with 3,044, so that, including wives and children, one could posit a population of 10,000–12,000. Which would nicely answer the problem of 7:4.[3]

Jerusalem, then, may be the holy city (vv. 1, 18) but it will not be worth much if it is an *empty* city. And that has been the concern of 11:3-24. The references to 'able men' (v. 6) and 'valiant warriors' (v. 14, so NASB) hint of a concern for military defense, if needed. They were a bit insecure about security.

If the city was not properly populated, not only would the city itself be vulnerable but so would the exercise of temple worship. There is an interesting petition in Psalm 84, a psalm reeking with passionate love for 'the courts of Yahweh.' In verses 8-9 the psalmist makes a petition: 'See our shield, O God; look on the face of your anointed' (v. 9). The 'shield' and 'anointed' are likely a reference to the reigning king. The worshiper asks Yahweh for favor and success for the king, because if the king fails or is defeated, the privilege of temple worship might go down the tube as well. The prosperity of the king is the necessary prerequisite for ongoing worship. This is analogous to what would happen on pay days in the parish of Kilbrandon and Kilchattan, in part of Scottish Argyllshire. Slate quarrying was a huge industry in the area in the late 1800s, and it was here that a highly respected Free Church minister, Donald MacDonald, served. The pastor was so concerned for his parishioners' welfare that on pay day at the quarries he would spend hours pacing up and down near the public house. His men so respected him that few would dare

---

3. Verses 20-24 tie up some loose ends. The king in verse 23 is likely the Persian king, who took an interest in the functioning of the temple worship (cf. Ezra 6:10; 7:23). Pethahiah (v. 24) was 'the king's liaison for Judean affairs' (Steinmann) and may well have usually resided at the Persian court.

to enter the pub to blow their money and their senses while he was there.[4] The minister's presence was a prerequisite for sobriety and solvency. So in the text. A population shift may seem a rather secular and mundane affair – yet essential, for it provides for the defensibility of the city and therefore for the security of temple worship.

The second head of this section can be called **possessing the land** (11:25-36). In this section we are away from Jerusalem and into the countryside, with a listing of places where Judah (vv. 25-30) and Benjamin (vv. 31-36) settled. These settlements stretch over quite an area. Kiriath-arba or Hebron is nineteen miles SSW of Jerusalem, Beersheba something like forty-five miles SW of Jerusalem, Ono to the northwest is a few miles east of Joppa on the coast. These locales may have gone beyond the confines of the Persian province of Yehud. 'But as citizens of the one empire, these people were free to settle where they would, provided they kept the peace.'[5] To get a graphic feel for these settlements, consult a good Bible atlas (e.g., Carl G. Rasmussen, *Zondervan NIV Atlas of the Bible* [1989], p. 144) and for clarification of the sites/locations, see Yamauchi, EBC, 4:546-49.

This section is not merely a bit of geography, however, but a chunk of theology. What stands behind Nehemiah 11 here is the place component of Yahweh's Abraham promise in Genesis 12! 'To your seed I will give this land' (Gen. 12:7). But Abraham's seed was wrenched out of this land, taken into exile, but now, at long last, Yahweh has brought them back to this land, and the people are beginning to sprinkle themselves over Abraham-turf once more. Oh, it's not very dramatic; it may seem pretty low-key – but it's significant all the same. It's like reading the last of the Samson story in Judges 16. Samson has been duped and decimated. Then you come to Judges 16:22, 'But the hair of his head began to grow again' (RSV). And you write in the margin of your Bible beside that verse, 'hmm ....' It's such a miniscule note and yet will turn out to be quite telling. And after the ruin and devastation of the exile to see these Jews back in the land and

---

4. Tom Lennie, *Glory in the Glen* (Ross-shire: Christian Focus, 2009), 55-56.

5. Derek Kidner, *Ezra and Nehemiah*, TOTC (Leicester: Inter-Varsity, 1979), 121.

beginning to possess it in small measure – clearly Yahweh has not cancelled the land promise.

I like the story William Barclay told of a London church having prepared for a harvest festival Sunday. But it was during 'the war.' And on the Saturday before came the first of the great blitzes and the harvest festival was never held because the church was a pile of ruins. On a table there had been sheaves of corn. Autumn came and passed, as did winter. Spring arrived and with it little green shoots all over the bomb site. Summer passed, autumn came, and on the bomb site was a flourishing patch of corn.[6] So don't despise a small, mustard-seed sort of beginning. Looking at a distance you may not think those folks settling around Adullam or in Anathoth are of much account. If so, you will have forgotten that Yahweh's promises pack a virile resilience.

The third segment in this order of the people of God deals with **structuring the worship** (12:1-26), and speaks of the provisions for such worship all the way from Zerubbabel to Nehemiah.[7] The text breaks down as follows:

- Priestly families and Levites at the time of Zerubbabel and Jeshua (*c.* 536 B.C.), vv. 1-9
- List of high priests, vv. 10-11[8]

---

6. William Barclay, *And Jesus Said* (Philadelphia: Westminster, 1970), 36.

7. Discussions of Nehemiah 12:1-26 can get terribly complex, especially in attempting to trace the proper historical background. Commentaries tend to offer more complexity than clarity. For the general reader, Mervin Breneman's treatment (*Ezra, Nehemiah, Esther*, NAC [n.p.: Broadman & Holman, 1993], 260-63) offers a straightforward explanation.

8. This list of high priests (12:10-11) has kept the ink industry from bankruptcy. The last listed, Jaddua, has garnered special attention. Josephus (*Antiquities*, 11:325-339) mentions a Jaddua as high priest when Alexander the Great came to Judea (*c.* 332 B.C.). Steinmann (*Ezra and Nehemiah*, CC [St. Louis: Concordia, 2010], 51-58) argues that the Jaddua of 12:11 is Josephus' Jaddua of *c.* 332 B.C., that the priestly listing here is a 'tight' listing (i.e., no gaps between generations), and so covers all the way from Jeshua (536 B.C.) to Jaddua in 332 B.C. This yields an average tenure of thirty-four years per high priest. Steinmann seems to think this is possible – and it is, but is, in my opinion, very unlikely. Moreover, it's risky to base anything on an identification by Josephus (unless one has additional evidence), for his account of matters in the Persian period are riddled with inaccuracies, as Steinmann himself takes pains to show. One doesn't have to accept the whole reconstruction of Frank Cross ('A Reconstruction of the Judean Restoration,' *Journal of Biblical Literature* 94 (1975): 4-18) to admit that the names of priests tended to recur in their descendants, i.e., papponymy, repeating the same name in alternate generations, so that grandsons are named after grandfathers. I take the

- Priests during Joiakim's time (second generation), vv. 12-21
- Notes about records, vv. 22-23
- Levites in Joiakim's time and following, vv. 24-26

At this point it is clear that everything for a re-ordered people of God has been touched upon:

- City, 11:1-24
- Land, 11:25-36
- Temple / worship, 12:1-26

What, however, is the *significance* of 12:1-26? What is it trying to tell us? I think we get a clue in the chronological references. The text begins (v. 1) with the time of Zerubbabel and Jeshua, the time of the return, roughly 538–533 B.C. Then the leaders of the priestly families are listed from 'the days of Joiakim' (v. 12), apparently the next generation after Zerubbabel and Jeshua. Then in verse 22 we find a reference to 'the days of Eliashib, Joiada, Johanan, and Jaddua' – high priests in the years after 'second generation' Joiakim. The text here is referring to when and where priestly and Levitical records were made. After this, in verses 24-25, we hear of Levites leading worship in the 'David tradition,' with verse 26 summarily speaking of the days of Joiakim all the way down and into 'the days of Nehemiah ... and Ezra ....' Aren't these notifications implying something like this: Folks are *still serving* in the worship of sacrifice and praise as did earlier generations. Is it not thrilling to see the true worship of God continuing in a subsequent generation? Isn't it marvelous to be a part of *a whole history of devotion* in one's own time? We are both non-biblical and ungrateful if we despise or ignore the record of those who have served Yahweh before our own time. In fact, that very realization may keep us faithful when under pressure to be faithless.

Jaddua of 12:11 to be an earlier one than the one alleged by Josephus, probably dating from around 400 B.C. I've omitted many details, e.g., whether the 'Jonathan' in the Hebrew text of 12:11 is the same as 'Johanan' in 12:22. Suffice to add I tend to think the 'Darius the Persian' in 12:22 is Darius II, 423–404 B.C.

This last was the case with Dr Wang, when the Boxers came after him in China about 1900. He was one of the first graduates from the Peking University Medical School. The Boxers arrested him along with his little son. They told him they didn't want to kill him but that if he didn't burn incense to the gods, they would have no choice. He refused. 'We'll make it easy for you. Get someone to burn incense in your place.' He still refused. They offered to find him a substitute and he'd only have to go along to the temple. His answer? 'No, I will not. You may kill me, but I will not worship your gods in any way. There are four generations of Christians in my family. Do you think I would let my child see his father deny his Savior?' They ran him through with a sword.[9] In his final words he implied, 'There is a *continuity* of devotion in my family. That has such a claim on me that I cannot betray it.' And so 'there shall be always a church on earth to worship God according to his will.'[10]

9. James and Marti Hefley, *By Their Blood*, 2nd. ed. (Grand Rapids: Baker, 1996), 38-39.

10. Westminster Confession of Faith, 25:5.

22

The Celebration in the Joy of the Lord
(Nehemiah 12:27–13:3)

Sometimes a celebration can be a bit delayed. Think of a married couple at their fiftieth wedding anniversary. Their family wants to celebrate the occasion but two daughters and one son (with their families) cannot mesh their schedules to get 'home' on the exact day. So the celebration may occur five weeks after the precise day. And, in Nehemiah, we are not sure how long after the completion of the wall (6:15) this dedication occurred. One has the impression that it took place after the events of chapters 7–11. It was not something to be neglected, but there may have been other, more pressing concerns (e.g., re-population, 11:1-2) at the very time when the wall was finished.

What then can one say about this special occasion? First of all, note that it was marked by **careful preparation** (12:27-30). Both personnel and purification were required. The former consisted of the Levites, especially those skilled in music and song. Some had to come from southeast of Bethlehem (Netophah), others from a bit north of Jerusalem in 'Benjaminite' territory (e.g., Geba, Azmaveth; vv. 27-29). And the priests and Levites seemed eager to carry out the necessary ritual purifications (v. 30). They purified themselves – and the people, gates, and wall. Exodus 19:10, 14-15 may give an idea of what personal purification involved. Purifying gates and a wall may be akin to purification of houses as in Leviticus

14:48-53, 'a ritual that included sprinkling with the blood of a sacrificial bird and fresh water using hyssop.'[1]

What's so impressive is how rigorously and diligently the people of Judah and their 'clergy' prepare for this occasion of celebration and worship. It is obviously a special occasion, but one wonders if their 'preparation' does not carry an implied rebuke for the contemporary church. Many churches make their pitch today to 'come as you are' (and I understand a partly laudable intent in that), but it seems to go beyond that. Churches work so hard to be *casual*, with coffee and donuts, multiple trips to the restroom during a service, 'fellowship' and chatter. Sometimes it almost seems like we're saying, 'Come as you are – we're only meeting with God, after all.'[2]

Second, note that **memorable processions** (vv. 31-43) form the very heart of the celebration. Nehemiah says that there on the top of the wall 'I appointed two large processions that gave thanks' (v. 31, HCSB). There is the first group, with Ezra (vv. 31-37), the second group that includes Nehemiah (vv. 38-39), while the goal was the temple (vv. 40-42). But the keynote of the occasion is the joy and gladness noted in verse 43. As many point out, there are five occurrences of the root *smh* (to be glad, rejoice) in that verse, as a pedantic rendering shows:

> Then they sacrificed on that day great sacrifices, and they were glad, because God had made them glad with great gladness, and even the women and children were glad, and the gladness of Jerusalem was heard a long way off.

I want to keep this keynote in view but go back over the text to see how this joy expresses itself and what feeds it.

It looks, first, as if joy *takes its time*. We've read enough of this document so far that we really shouldn't be shocked that Nehemiah goes into list mode. Impatient Westerners that we are, we may wonder why we need the names of seven who followed along with Hoshaiah (vv. 32-34). And why does the

---

1. Andrew E. Steinmann, *Ezra and Nehemiah*, CC (St. Louis: Concordia, 2010), 592.

2. Note, in light of verse 43, that such seriousness and preparation is not the enemy of joy but its companion.

son of a priest, Zechariah, have to have his six-step pedigree spelled out (v. 35; well, maybe the link with Asaph?), and why do we need eight of his 'brothers' listed in detail (v. 36)? They arrive at the temple, and it looks like we have about fifteen priests listed by name (vv. 41-42). Does it matter that Micaiah and Elioenai are there? Will we be likely to remember Azarel, Milalai, and Gilalai as Zechariah's kinsmen (v. 36)? Why this slow-paced, seemingly tedious listing of all these people? Why can't the Bible just get on with it?

Because joy is not in a hurry. It savors each servant who was there – hence the names. It takes the time to dwell on them, write down their names, give them their place. Joy revels in the details and increases as it takes time to remember. I've used gastronomical analogies before. I have a friend in Mississippi who would make the most luscious banana pudding, fill an almost mini-vat with it, and bring it to monthly church dinners. While most all were working their way through the line for the main courses, I would go to the dessert table and help myself to a generous bowl of said pudding, at which point one had to remember proper technique. One doesn't simply shovel it in, gobble it down. No, you must, well, 'care' for it, take your time with it, savor it, take a bite and swish it around through your teeth. Joy comes by being deliberate with it. That, I think, is what Nehemiah is doing with this very relaxed and detailed account of the wall dedication.

A second point is that joy *covets memories*. Just for a moment, let me allude to the apparent procedure atop the wall. It seems that the two groups must have been somewhere around the Valley Gate on the west of the city, and that Ezra and his group went to the south (v. 31) and the other went to the north (v. 38). There are quite a number of specific 'stops' noted in the journey of this second group (vv. 38-39).[3] Can you imagine how this 'walking the wall' must have flooded many of these former builders with memories? One elbows a fellow marcher as they approach the Dung Gate and says, 'Remember how it took us two days just to clear the rubble off

---

3. Readers may find it useful to consult again the sketch provided with Nehemiah 3.

this place?' Others might rehearse how it took three of them to get a contrary stone in place near the Tower of the Ovens. Places tend to etch themselves in our memories. I doubt, for example, that C. S. Lewis ever forgot Whipsnade Zoo. He recalled that sunny morning when they left for it: 'When we set out I did not believe that Jesus Christ is the Son of God, and when we reached the zoo I did.'[4] Tends to make one remember a zoo.

These processions, then, rivet their minds and imaginations to the work and pain and ordeal they had endured – such processions can become an act of worship. The purpose of it all was thanksgiving. But circling the wall added concreteness and vividness – and joy (v. 43) – to this thanksgiving.

The third note of this occasion has to do with **scriptural fidelity** (12:44-47; 13:1-3). Here are two sections of 'footnotes' attached to the wall celebration. 'On that day' in 12:43 is picked up by the same phrasing in 12:44 and 13:1, so binding these two 'footnote' segments to the wall celebration account.[5] Israel's conduct in both episodes comes as an obedient response to the torah (12:44; 13:3). They did what they did because Scripture told them to do so.

The first segment (12:44-47) deals with *provision* – provision for those serving in the temple worship. The joy and delight in those who led in worship (v. 44b) led to action meant to insure the ongoing continuity of worship. Men were appointed to see that the pledges of 10:35-39 were actually carried out. These contributions, first fruits, and tithes were for the support of the priests and Levites and for the singers and gatekeepers. And the Levites themselves offered a tithe of their portions to the priests (v. 47; cf. Num. 18:21-29).

There was evidently quite an enthusiasm for this task, at least initially (v. 44b). But God's people must constantly keep a finger on their pulse, for we are sometimes prone to enjoy dramatic celebrations (like 12:27-43) and yet neglect the ordinary dog-duties that torah also requires. 'It is one thing to shout on a great occasion, but another to offer the

---

4. C. S. Lewis, *Surprised by Joy* (New York: Harcourt Brace Jovanovich, 1955), 237.

5. I am not convinced by Steinmann's (pp. 602-03) attempt to pry 13:1-3 loose from the preceding context.

sacrifice of praise continually and to make realistic provision for the church's needs.'[6] So here we are taught the importance of ongoing, non-special obedience. It is easy to neglect or despise this. Paul Johnson has an interesting assessment of Leo Tolstoy in this regard. Tolstoy, he says, was willing to make a great sacrifice, 'provided it could be done as a grand, theatrical gesture, and everyone noticed.' It was always that way – heroism and virtue were for public consumption, 'not for the dull, unrecorded routine of everyday life.' The way he viewed his multiple gambling debts was a case in point. Apparently, at a later point, he renounced gambling, but felt no concern to re-pay his many lenders, some of them poor men. 'There was nothing dramatic about paying an old debt.'[7] Genuine faith will always rejoice to practice the more plodding kind of obedience.

The second segment focuses on *separation* (13:1-3). The text the people heard was Deuteronomy 23:3-6. They heard the text (vv. 1-2); then they applied the text to their contemporary situation (v. 3). Apparently they 'principalized' from the required exclusion of Ammonites and Moabites in the ancient text and deduced that the text demanded the exclusion of 'all foreigners' (v. 3).

Now if a modern reader happened by chance to read this text in Nehemiah, he or she might go into orbit. But before we deal with the 'obnoxiousness' of this text, let's notice the underlying assumption that governs it. Why this severe sanction against Ammonites and Moabites? Because they ignored the needs of God's people and also laid hold of Balaam, the prophetic 'hired gun,' to put the hoky-poky and curse on Israel. You see the implication? It is a perilous matter to disdain and assault the people of God. It brings dire consequences. It is a lesson that jihadists and Islamic terrorists and military juntas and godless dictators have yet to learn in our day.

But what about the sentimentalists or militants who would either whine or rage about this exclusive separation? They would look at 13:1-3 and ask why these Judeans were

---

6. Derek Kidner, *Ezra and Nehemiah*, TOTC (Leicester: Inter-Varsity, 1979), 127.

7. Paul Johnson, *Intellectuals* (New York: Harper & Row, 1990), 111, 115.

so arrogant that they could not embrace people of differing 'perspectives.' Where is the respect for diversity? Isn't this just like 'the God of the Old Testament'? Why are these people driven by such a narrow paganphobia?[8]

Answer: because it's a matter of life and death. There was a Jewish colony at Elephantine in Egypt contemporary with Ezra and Nehemiah. Papyri from there reveal the practice of mixed marriages. There's one document that offers the salutation: 'I bless you by Yaho [Yahweh] and by Khnub [the Egyptian god]!'[9] The Jews there had a temple where sacrifices were offered to Yahweh, but, as John Bright notes, other divine beings were also worshiped, e.g., Eshem-bethel, Herem-bethel, Anath-bethel. Bright then summarizes:

> It appears from this that the Jews of Elephantine, if not overtly polytheists, had combined a highly unorthodox Yahwism with features drawn from syncretistic cults of Aramean origin. Though calling themselves Jews and feeling kinship, as we shall see, with their brethren in Palestine, they by no means stood in the mainstream of Israel's history and faith.[10]

That's what happens when a people is 'open to diversity.' Covenant people disappear, washed down into the sewer line of history. So a proper biblical 'separation' is urgent. Bear in mind now Ezra 6:21 – there was a way for foreigners to come among the people of God provided they became disciples of Yahweh. But otherwise God's people must maintain a sort of in-your-face separation, whether it be in doctrine or ethics and morality or in the face of the prevailing mind-sets of this age. Of course, sanctification will often appear obnoxious to the world; but it's all right – they have to have something to stew about.

---

8. This is what is so lovable about the Bible – it simply stiff-arms the gospels of secular culture.

9. Edwin M. Yamauchi, *Persia and the Bible* (Grand Rapids: Baker, 1990), 245.

10. John Bright, *A History of Israel*, 3rd ed. (Philadelphia: Westminster, 1981), 376.

23

Is Reformation Really Possible?
Or: The Ongoing Perils of the Church
(Nehemiah 13:4-31)

There is a conundrum at the beginning of 13:4. The opening phrase is almost uniformly translated in a temporal sense, e.g., as NASB, 'Now prior to this.' This implies that the following episode in which the priest Eliashib gave Tobiah motel accommodations in the temple took place before at least the episode of 13:1-3. But the two sections 12:44-47 and 13:1-3 both began with 'In that day' and most naturally refer to the time of the wall dedication. Nehemiah was clearly present at that time. However, 13:6 implies that the reason Eliashib checked Tobiah into temple quarters was because Nehemiah was gone, apparently on leave, reporting back to the king. Though I have found no one else who holds it, I prefer Howard Crosby's suggestion in *Lange's Commentary* that the initial phrase (*weliphney mizzeh,* found nowhere else in the Old Testament) should be rendered, 'in the presence of this,' carrying the sense of 'in the face of it all,' as if to say: In spite of the celebration and reforms noted in 12:27–13:3, Eliashib dared to introduce Tobiah into the temple chambers – and did this while Nehemiah was back in Persia (cf. v. 6). On this view the phrase introduces an act of defiance by Eliashib.[1] In any case, this last major section of Nehemiah

---

1. Greg Goswell offers another possibility (*A Study Commentary on Ezra–Nehemiah* [Darlington: EP Books, 2013], 348). If I understand him correctly, he

contains a veritable catalog of the perils of the people of God, beginning with Eliashib's fiasco.

The first peril is **compromise** (vv. 4-9). Whether the Eliashib here is a 'regular' priest or the high priest (v. 28) doesn't matter. It's as though, if we take Crosby's view (above), there is that note of defiance in his coddling of Tobiah. Then Eliashib would be flying in the teeth of the reform of verses 1-3, which excluded Ammonites among others – and Tobiah was an Ammonite.

The *ease* of compromise is clear in verse 4b: Eliashib was 'near to Tobiah.' This may mean he was closely associated with him, or perhaps related to him (Tobiah had marriage ties in Judah anyway, cf. 6:17-19). For Eliashib, camaraderie trumps covenant. Eliashib thought pleasing man matters more than fidelity to God.

The *opportunity* for compromise was the absence of Nehemiah (v. 6). The thirty-second year of Artaxerxes would have been 433 B.C. If Nehemiah came to Jerusalem in 445, he then had been there some twelve years. Now he takes a hiatus. Who know how long – some months, a year, whatever (and returns later). Here is where one discovers the depth of fidelity. Does it rest only on someone's external presence (Nehemiah's, in this case)? Does our faithfulness evaporate when the external restraint is not there (as did Eliashib's)? Or is our fidelity internally driven?

The *cure* for compromise is the return of Nehemiah (vv. 7-9)! Eviction was the answer. Nehemiah threw Tobiah's furniture and his boxer shorts and T-shirts and dresser drawers and mattresses out on the curb (kerb) for Wednesday trash pick up. The compromise of Eliashib was in opposition to the Word of God (see vv. 1-3), and therefore, it must be dealt with precipitously instead of gently. There are times when gentleness is sin. Ask Eli (1 Sam. 2:22-29).

The next peril is **neglect** or **indifference** (vv. 10-14). The Levites were to live on tithes that were given (Num. 18:21), but these had not been given them, the procedures of 12:44-47 having gone into eclipse. Hence the Levites had 'fled' to the

---

translates the phrase 'Earlier' but thinks it does not refer backward but forward, as if there's a sort of ellipsis till verse 6, so that it carries the idea 'this happened earlier during the time when I was gone.'

towns and to their fields to gather what living they could there. So the house of God was 'forsaken' (v. 11; cf. 10:39). Who knows what Nehemian pressure may lurk behind verse 12! It simply reports, 'All Judah then brought the tithe of the grain, wine, and oil into the storehouses' (NASB). So obedience is re-activated. And to attempt to ensure the system from (further) breakdown, Nehemiah appointed reliable men over this business (v. 13).

Here again is one of Nehemiah's prayers in verse 14. Once again, this is not a works-merit prayer. It is a prayer in the spirit of Hebrews 6:10, Mark 14:9, and Matthew 10:40-42. It is the prayer of one who knows God does not ignore the earnest service of unworthy servants. Nehemiah asks that God not wipe out his 'loyal deeds' (NASB). The term is the plural form of *hesed*, used of Yahweh's 'covenant love' or 'steadfast love.' Nehemiah's deeds then are those done out of a covenant commitment, deeds of steadfast love done in response to Yahweh's steadfast love.

The third peril in the text is **commercialism** (vv. 15-22). The problem here has to do with the sabbath. The *offense* was double: the people of Judah were working on the sabbath, bringing loads of foodstuffs into Jerusalem and (apparently) selling them (v. 15); then there were the foreigners, the Tyrians, who didn't give a rip about the sabbath and who did their fish-selling on the sabbath (v. 16).

Nehemiah's *rebuke* or *argument* is a theological one (vv. 17-18): these sabbath-breakers are placing Israel under the anger of Yahweh again. See this argument pressed by the prophet Jeremiah in the pre-exilic period (Jer. 17:19-27). *Prevention* consisted in closing and guarding the city gates. Nehemiah placed his own men there to prevent traders from entering the city (v. 19b). Then he made threats against the lollygaggers in verses 20-21. Perhaps these tried to hang around outside the walls hoping to attract people to come out of the city to buy. But Nehemiah shuts this off. His threats are never empty (v. 21)! Then in verse 22 he institutes a more lasting provision to ensure compliance.

At this point I think it well if we go on a short tangent about the sabbath. Tangents aren't bad as long as you know you are on one and eventually get off it. So a bit about *the background and theology of the sabbath.* This will likely make some readers angry, others disappointed, and still others thinking there is need for more depth. I realize there are debates about linking the sabbath and 'the Lord's Day,' and that there are some who likely regard the sabbath as more of a ceremonial affair for Israel. However, I cannot escape the fact that the sabbath idea seems written into creation (Gen. 2:1-3) and was a 'live' matter even before Sinai (cf. Exod. 16).

Exodus 31:12-17 indicates (especially verses 13 and 17) that the sabbath is a 'sign.' It marked Israel out as unique, for other peoples did not have the sabbath. Strangely, perhaps in reaction to later scribal details and legalism, there is often a negative view of the sabbath in the contemporary church. Even evangelicalism, though holding a kind of tolerance for the sabbath, has more interest in bolstering the case for why we don't need to adhere to the fourth commandment. For some, there are only nine commandments.

But note Exodus 20:8-11. The sabbath is a gift because God's people *shabat* on it, they *stop* work (Exod. 34:21). Only a free people does that. Only a free people can do that. In Egypt they dare not have stopped work! But when Yahweh frees from bondage he enables them to cease from incessant work. Every week! The sabbath is a sign of grace and freedom, not of bondage. *Slaves* work all the time, but *free people* have the liberty of rest – including servants and livestock and sojourners! Here is the *social* benefit of the commandment. So when you insist on cluttering the sabbath with work …

1. It is a *failure of faith,* because by your working and not 'stopping,' you are saying that you cannot trust Yahweh to provide for you but must keep working because all your life rests on your efforts.

2. It is a *failure of compassion,* because then your dependents (family, servants, livestock) will not enjoy rest. See Deuteronomy 5:14 for this social argument.

3. It is a *choice of bondage,* for you are deifying work, subjecting yourself to a continuous treadmill which Yahweh meant to interrupt weekly. But you are saying, 'No, I *want* to be a slave, I want to return to Egypt; I want to run, frustrated and exhausted, to Walmart

and Target, to the grocery store and pharmacy, on the Lord's Day. I want to pay bills then, I want to complete seminary assignments then, I want to wash my car and mow my lawn and work on my income tax and go to the car dealership – I want to *be a slave!* I do not want rest or quietness or solitude – I might meet God.'

Yahweh's pattern is: work six days and stop. It is a way of saying that work is not god. These principles remain for the people of God, even though our culture and government is non-covenantal and pays no attention to them.

Now, from tangent back to text. The fourth peril here is **amalgamation** (vv. 23-31). Here we go ... intermarriage again.

Here note the *drift* to be seen in the second generation (vv. 23-24). Intermarriage with pagans occurs (v. 23) and one discovers that the cultural ties of the children are closer to the (pagan) mothers' roots (v. 24); eventually this will prove true for religious ties as well. 'A single generation's compromise could undo the work of centuries.'[2]

Note the *action* taken (v. 25). Looks like Nehemiah engaged in a bit of gubernatorial intimidation! Among other things, he 'cursed them.' What does that mean? Fensham explains:

> Nehemiah cursed them, not in the modern sense of the word, but in terms of the pronouncement of a religious curse. In Neh. 10 the forming of a covenant is described with the stipulation that foreign marriages are out. If the covenant should be broken, the religious curse would come into effect. This is what we have here.[3]

Then Nehemiah makes these folks take an oath to not give their daughters in marriage to pagans nor to take pagan women in marriage for their sons (v. 25b). This was what they *had already sworn* not to do in 10:28-30!

Nehemiah presses an *argument* upon them, a biblical-theological-historical argument, based on King Solomon's drift toward paganism (vv. 26-27). He enjoyed vast privileges but came to ruin because of this very offense (see 1 Kings 11:1-13).

---

2. Derek Kidner, *Ezra and Nehemiah*, TOTC (Leicester: Inter-Varsity, 1979), 131.

3. F. Charles Fensham, *The Books of Ezra and Nehemiah*, NICOT (Grand Rapids: Eerdmans, 1982), 267.

But here, currently, in Judah, there was an *aggravation* of the offense: marriages to pagans had occurred among the priestly circles of the community (vv. 28-29). It was not simply a problem among the 'lay' people – religious leaders of the community were guilty of this crime. The grandson of the high priest, Eliashib, had married the daughter of Sanballat the Horonite.

> Lev. 21:14 prohibits the high priest from marrying a foreigner. Any person in the high-priestly lineage could become high priest. On the other hand, Sanballat was the archenemy of Nehemiah. Such an act as that of Eliashib's grandson was a direct challenge to the authority of Nehemiah. So it was regarded as the highest form of religious apostasy. Nehemiah *chased him* away, which means that Nehemiah expelled him from the Jewish religious community.[4]

So it was that bad. A grandson of the high priest son-in-law to Sanballat! How to deal with that? In Nehemiah style: Lit., 'I made him flee away from me' (v. 28b). He can go live with the syncretists.

I suppose some modern readers are aghast at Nehemiah's reactions in verse 25: he cursed them, struck some of them, pulled out their hair! You didn't mess with Nehemiah. We aren't obligated to justify every response Nehemiah made, but wouldn't it drive one half-mad if, after some years of Ezra's teaching and Nehemiah's leadership, one sees their people stepping into the same cesspool again? Sometimes strong reactions are called for.

During the Great Depression socialist and communist propaganda made its rounds in the United States. Even in parts of the Deep South. Bethel Baptist Church in Birmingham, Alabama, located in a mainly African-American neighborhood, had its share of controversy. Some of its members in the 1930s were communist activists; the pastor, Milton Sears, was intensely anti-communist. On one occasion Sears helped police find an accused black suspect in a criminal investigation – that drew the ire of many African-Americans and also of Communist Party activists.

---

4. ibid.

Communists circulated propaganda against Sears. When a communist-led crowd rose up against Sears during a service, Pastor Sears pulled out a shotgun and 'drove his antagonists from the sanctuary.'[5] Sometimes dire recourses are necessary.

That is the idea operating in the text. The point of verses 23-31 surely is that *emergency conditions call for extreme measures* (a principle, by the way, enunciated by Jesus in Matthew 5:29-30). Remember that the amalgamation of the present-day people of God also occurs precisely here: intermarriage with ungodly, unconverted spouses.

Now let's step back from 13:4-31 and take an overview of it again. Here Nehemiah relates the work he had to do:

> Purging impurity, vv. 4-9
> Renewing the tithe, vv. 10-14
> Enforcing the sabbath, vv. 15-22
> Disciplining the unfaithful, vv. 23-29

Do you see now what Nehemiah 13 is saying? Note that the four abuses above corrected by Nehemiah had *already been eschewed in the covenant of 10:30-39.* In light of this, I want you to ponder two quotations, which, I believe, are on the mark:

> The final note in Ezra-Nehemiah is thus one of ambiguity. We may wonder how the people who had so exuberantly celebrated the completion of the defences against the enemy came so readily to accept the enemy's presence within the Temple and the high priest's family. How, indeed, could those who had committed themselves so solemnly to religious purity (chapter 10) so rapidly return to practices which were essentially irreligious? If we sense a certain desperation about Nehemiah's last efforts to put the house of Israel in order, a tiredness about the need yet again to bring back the wandering sheep to the right path, a feeling that there is no reason to think that this reform will be more successful than any other, a sense that after all he himself has done his best (vv. 14, 22b, 31b), then we may be catching the right meaning here.[6]

---

5. Thomas S. Kidd, *American History, Volume 2* (Nashville: B & H Academic, 2019), 147.

6. J. G. McConville, *Ezra, Nehemiah, and Esther*, The Daily Study Bible (Philadelphia: Westminster, 1985), 149.

And then:

> The Book of Nehemiah seems to peter out in what might be considered a somewhat unsatisfactory manner, not so much with a bang as with a whimper. All the abuses referred to in this final chapter have been the subject of earlier treatment, but they rear their heads again here despite the best efforts of the reformers to eradicate them .... It is as though the book is pointing to its own failure, reminding us that however important good structures and routines may be ..., nothing can substitute for the renewal of the naturally perverse inclinations of the human heart.[7]

Those estimates do not discount the labors of Ezra and Nehemiah but expose the flakiness of the professing people of God. Does not the end of Ezra–Nehemiah then function as a blinking, yellow caution-light to those who place too much confidence in reform of the church? Not that such reform should not be pressed. It should. But can't there sometimes be a subtle arrogance in it? 'We will separate from such-and-such a body, and we will start a new denomination, and we will see to it that it remains confessionally orthodox, fosters godly piety, and never gets on the slippery slope to compromise.' But, probably, it will, eventually. Not even among the people of God can irreversible constancy be found, not even when they take sacred vows to remain faithful (chapter 10). Do you see how Ezra–Nehemiah preaches an *implicit messianism*? Does not the failure of Israel in this Scripture make you look for the Israelite who will not fail? Covenants are solemnly sworn yet easily broken. Where will one find the Covenant-keeper except in our faithful Savior, Jesus Christ? Ezra–Nehemiah should drum into us a holy distrust of ourselves, even in our most 'committed' moments, and give us a clear grasp of how tenuous our devotion is.

> Prone to wander, Lord, I feel it;
> Prone to leave the God I love.[8]

Isn't it healthy to see that? And if we do, is there not hope?

---

7. H. G. M. Williamson, 'Ezra and Nehemiah,' in *New Bible Commentary*, 4th ed. (Leicester: Inter-Varsity, 1994), 440.

8. From the hymn 'Come, Thou Fount of Every Blessing,' by Robert Robinson, in stanza 3.

Subject Index

Y

Z

Scripture Index

Christian Focus Publications

Our mission statement
Staying Faithful

In dependence upon God we seek to impact the world through literature faithful to His infallible Word, the Bible. Our aim is to ensure that the Lord Jesus Christ is presented as the only hope to obtain forgiveness of sin, live a useful life and look forward to heaven with Him.

Our Books are published in four imprints:

◁OX CHRISTIAN FOCUS

Popular works including biographies, commentaries, basic doctrine and Christian living.

◁OX MENTOR

Books written at a level suitable for Bible College and seminary students, pastors, and other serious readers. The imprint includes commentaries, doctrinal studies, examination of current issues and church history.

◁OX CHRISTIAN HERITAGE

Books representing some of the best material from the rich heritage of the church.

◁OX CF4KIDS

Children's books for quality Bible teaching and for all age groups: Sunday school curriculum, puzzle and activity books; personal and family devotional titles, biographies and inspirational stories – because you are never too young to know Jesus!

Christian Focus Publications Ltd,
Geanies House, Fearn, Ross-shire,
IV20 1TW, Scotland, United Kingdom.
www.christianfocus.com